HE'S NOT THROUGH WITH YOU YET
IT'S A PROCESS

BY:KERRYANN MCBEAN

Copyright © 2025 by Kerryann Mcbean

All rights reserved. No part of this book may be used or reproduced in any form whatsoever without written permission except in the case of brief quotations in critical articles or reviews.

Printed in the United States of America/ Canada.

For more information, or to book an event, contact :
Email Info@cojbookz.com

ISBN - Paperback: 978-1-998120-68-0

" Processing Is Necessary For The Journey With God"

Kerryann Mcbean

CONTENTS

Acknowledgments	7
1 Understanding the Process	8
2 God's Purpose for Your Life	14
3 Waiting on God	20
4 Faith Over Fear	25
5 The Role of Trials	30
6 Breaking and Molding	35
7 Seasons of Silence	41
8 Spiritual Warfare	48
9 Surrender and Obedience	54
10 The Power of Prayer and Worship	61
11 Healing from the Past	68
12 The Renewing of the Mind	76
13 Walking in Your Calling	84
14 Overcoming Setbacks	93

15 The Importance of Community	102
16 Endurance and Perseverance	109
17 Living a Life of Faith	114
18 God's Timing is Perfect	121
19 The Power of Testimony	125
20 He's Not Through with You Yet	131

Acknowledgement:

I want to acknowledge my sister, Yvonne Francis, she was the one to whom the Holy Spirit gave the title of this book while she was praying at midnight in December of 2024. May the Lord continue to bless and keep her as she continues to seek the face of God.

Love, your sister Kerryann.

CHAPTER 1

Understanding the Process

Introduction

Have you ever wondered why God doesn't just fix everything in your life instantly? Why does He allow you to endure difficulties, setbacks, and long seasons of waiting? The answer is simple: God works through a process.

Everything God does is intentional, and He often leads us through stages of growth, refinement, and preparation before fulfilling His promises in our lives. Understanding that life is a process—and that God is in control of it—helps us develop patience, faith, and trust in Him.

God's Process Is Not Instant, but It Is Perfect

We live in a world of instant gratification. We want quick results, immediate success, and fast solutions. However, God doesn't work on human timelines. Instead, He takes us through a process to shape us, strengthen us, and prepare us for the future.

Example: Joseph's Journey

One of the greatest biblical examples of God's process is Joseph.

- Dream at 17 (Genesis 37:5-11): God gave Joseph a vision of leadership, but he was young, inexperienced, and not ready to fulfill it.

- Betrayal and Slavery (Genesis 37:18-28): His own brothers sold him into slavery, an event that seemed like a terrible setback.

- False Accusation and Prison (Genesis 39:6-20): He was falsely accused and imprisoned for years.

- God's Favor in the Waiting (Genesis 39:21-23): Even in prison, Joseph remained faithful, and God was with him.

- Promotion to Power (Genesis 41:39-41): After 13 years of trials, Joseph was placed in a position of great leadership in Egypt.

Joseph's journey teaches us that the process is necessary for the promise. If God had placed Joseph in leadership immediately, he would not have had the wisdom, humility, and strength needed to lead an entire nation.

Key Scripture:

"Being confident of this, that He who began a good work in you will carry it on to completion until the day of Christ Jesus." – Philippians 1:6

God doesn't start something in your life only to abandon you halfway. If He began a good work in you, He will finish it.

Three Key Truths About God's Process

1. God Uses the Process to Prepare You

Before God places you in your calling, He equips you. Every hardship, lesson, and delay is shaping you for the future.

Scripture:

"For you have need of endurance, so that after you have done the will of God, you may receive the promise." – Hebrews 10:36

2. Delays Are Not Denials

Sometimes, God's timing doesn't align with our expectations. But a delay does not mean God has said no. He may simply be working behind the scenes.

Example: Abraham and Sarah waited 25 years for the promise of Isaac (Genesis 21:1-2). Their waiting wasn't wasted—God was working.

Scripture:

"Wait for the Lord; be strong and take heart and wait for the Lord." – Psalm 27:14

3. The Process Builds Your Character

God is more interested in who you become than in what you achieve. The process refines your faith, humbles your heart, and teaches you to depend on Him.

Scripture:

"Consider it pure joy, my brothers and sisters, whenever you face trials of many kinds, because you know that the testing of your faith produces perseverance. Let perseverance finish its work so that you may be mature and complete, not lacking anything." – James 1:2-4

Personal Reflection Questions

1. Can you identify a season in your life when you went through a process that later made sense?

2. How does understanding that "delays are not denials" change your perspective on waiting?

3. What is one area in your life where you feel stuck? How might God be using this season for your growth?

Application: How to Trust the Process

1. Stay Faithful Where You Are

Joseph remained faithful in every season, even when things didn't make sense. Serve God where you are today.

Scripture:

"Whatever you do, work at it with all your heart, as working for the Lord, not for human masters." – Colossians 3:23

2. Strengthen Your Faith Through Prayer

Pray for wisdom and patience. Ask God to help you trust His timing.

Scripture:

"Trust in the Lord with all your heart and lean not on your own understanding; in all your ways submit to Him, and He will make your paths straight." – Proverbs 3:5-6

3. Remember That God's Plan Is Always Good

Even when you don't understand it, God's plan is for your good.

Scripture:

"'For I know the plans I have for you,' declares the Lord, 'plans to prosper you and not to harm you, plans to give you hope and a future.'" – Jeremiah 29:11

Study Guide: "Understanding the Process"

Memory Verse: Philippians 1:6

"He who began a good work in you will carry it on to completion."

Daily Reading Plan:

- Day 1: Genesis 37 – Joseph's dreams and betrayal
- Day 2: Genesis 39 – Joseph's faithfulness in trials
- Day 3: Genesis 41 – Joseph's promotion
- Day 4: James 1:2-4 – Trials and perseverance
- Day 5: Proverbs 3:5-6 – Trusting God's process

Discussion Questions:

1. What are some signs that God is taking you through a process?
2. How can trials shape your character and faith?
3. How can you encourage someone else who is struggling in their waiting season?

Conclusion: Trust the Process

God's work in your life is not random; it is intentional. You may not see the full picture now but trust that He is shaping you for something greater. The key is to remain faithful, trust in His timing, and believe that He is not through with you yet!

CHAPTER 2

God's Purpose for Your Life

Have you ever asked, "Why am I here?" or "What is my purpose?" Many people struggle with these questions, feeling lost or unsure of their calling. The good news is that God created you with a purpose—a divine reason for your existence.

Finding your purpose isn't about chasing success or pleasing people. It's about discovering God's plan and aligning your life with His will. In this chapter, we'll explore how to recognize and walk in your God-given purpose.

1. You Were Created for a Purpose

God doesn't create anything without intention. You are not an accident—you were designed for a specific reason.

Scripture:

"For we are God's handiwork, created in Christ Jesus to do good works, which God prepared in advance for us to do." – Ephesians 2:10

This verse tells us three important truths:

1. You are God's handiwork – You were intentionally designed by Him.
2. You were created in Christ – Your identity and purpose are found in Jesus.

3. You were made for good works – God has already prepared things for you to accomplish.

Example: Jeremiah's Calling

Before Jeremiah was even born, God had a purpose for him:

"Before I formed you in the womb, I knew you, before you were born, I set you apart; I appointed you as a prophet to the nations." – Jeremiah 1:5

Just like Jeremiah, God has a plan for your life—even if you don't fully understand it yet.

2. Your Purpose is Connected to God, Not Just Your Talents

Many people assume their skills, talents, or careers define their purpose. While these can be part of God's plan, your true purpose is always rooted in your relationship with Him.

Example: Paul's Transformation

Before Paul became a great apostle, he was Saul—a man who persecuted Christians. Yet, when Paul encountered Jesus, his entire purpose changed (Acts 9:1-19). His new mission was to spread the Gospel, not just to use his skills.

Your purpose is not just about what you do—it's about who you serve.

Key Scripture:

"Commit to the Lord whatever you do, and He will establish your plans." – Proverbs 16:3

When you commit your life to God, He will direct your steps toward your purpose.

3. Recognizing Your Purpose

If you're unsure of your purpose, ask yourself:

- •What gifts and passions has God given me?
- •What opportunities has He placed before me?
- •What burdens do I feel strongly about?

Example: Moses felt a strong burden for the suffering of his people (Exodus 3:7-10). That burden was connected to his purpose—to lead the Israelites out of Egypt.

God often places a desire or passion in your heart as a clue to what He is calling you to do.

Key Scripture:

"Delight yourself in the Lord, and He will give you the desires of your heart." – Psalm 37:4

When you seek God, He aligns your heart's desires with His will.

4. Walking in Your Purpose Requires Faith

Even when God reveals your purpose, the journey may not be easy. It takes faith, perseverance, and trust in God's timing.

Example: Esther's Boldness

Esther didn't know her full purpose until she was placed in a position to save her people. She had to step out in faith and courage to fulfill her calling (Esther 4:14-16).

Like Esther, God may be preparing you for "such a time as this"—even if you don't fully see it yet.

Personal Reflection Questions

1. What talents, passions, or burdens has God placed in your heart?
2. Are there any areas where you feel stuck in discovering your purpose?
3. How can you seek God more to gain clarity about His plan for you?

Application: How to Walk in Your Purpose

1. Seek God First

You will never fully understand your purpose apart from God. Spend time in prayer, reading the Bible, and listening for His guidance.

Scripture:

"But seek first His kingdom and His righteousness, and all these things will be given to you as well." – Matthew 6:33

2. Take Small Steps of Faith

You may not see the whole picture yet, but start where you are. Serve God with what you have, and He will lead you forward.

Scripture:

"Your word is a lamp for my feet, a light on my path." – Psalm 119:105

A lamp only lights the next few steps—trust God for the next move.

3. Trust God's Timing

You may feel like you're behind or that things aren't moving fast enough, but God's timing is perfect.

Scripture:

"There is a time for everything and a season for every activity under the heavens." – Ecclesiastes 3:1

Study Guide: "God's Purpose for Your Life"

Memory Verse: Ephesians 2:10

"For we are God's handiwork, created in Christ Jesus to do good works, which God prepared in advance for us to do."

Daily Reading Plan:

- Day 1: Jeremiah 1 – God's plan for Jeremiah
- Day 2: Acts 9 – Paul's transformation
- Day 3: Esther 4 – Esther's calling and boldness
- Day 4: Exodus 3 – Moses' burden and calling
- Day 5: Proverbs 16:3 – Trusting God with your plans

Discussion Questions:

1. Have you ever felt a strong burden for something? Could it be connected to your purpose?

2.What is one step of faith you can take toward discovering or fulfilling your purpose?

3.How can you trust God more in seasons of uncertainty about your calling?

Conclusion: Your Purpose is in God's Hands

You don't have to figure everything out on your own. God has a plan for you, and he will reveal it in His perfect time. Stay faithful, seek Him first, and trust that He is leading you toward your purpose!

Now that we've discussed purpose, the next challenge is waiting on God's timing.

CHAPTER 3

Waiting On God

Waiting is one of the hardest parts of the Christian journey. When we don't see immediate answers to our prayers, it's easy to feel frustrated, discouraged, or even forgotten by God. However, waiting is part of the process. God's timing is perfect, and during seasons of waiting, He is working behind the scenes, refining us, and preparing us for what's ahead.

In this chapter, we will explore why God sometimes asks us to wait, what we should do in the waiting season, and how to trust Him fully.

1. Why Does God Make Us Wait?

1.1. To Build Our Faith

Faith is trusting in what we cannot see. If God answered every prayer instantly, we would never learn to trust Him.

Scripture:

"Now faith is the confidence in what we hope for and assurance about what we do not see." – Hebrews 11:1

1.2. To Develop Our Character

Waiting refines us. It teaches patience, endurance, and humility.

Scripture:

"We also glory in our sufferings, because we know that suffering produces perseverance; perseverance, character; and character, hope." – Romans 5:3-4

1.3. To Prepare Us for the Next Season

Sometimes, we are not yet ready for what we are praying for. God is developing the skills, wisdom, and strength we will need for the next level.

Example: David – David was anointed king as a young shepherd (1 Samuel 16:13), but he didn't become king until years later. In the waiting, he learned leadership, patience, and trust in God.

2. What Should We Do While We Wait?

2.1. Keep Praying and Seeking God

Instead of giving up, continue seeking God daily.

Scripture:

"Rejoice always, pray without ceasing, give thanks in all circumstances; for this is the will of God in Christ Jesus for you." – 1 Thessalonians 5:16-18

2.2. Stay Faithful in Small Things

While waiting, be diligent in what God has already placed in front of you. Be faithful in the little things, and God will open bigger doors.

Scripture:

"Whoever can be trusted with very little can also be trusted with much." – Luke 16:10

2.3. Trust That God's Timing Is Best

We may not understand God's timing, but He is never late.

Scripture:

"There is a time for everything, and a season for every activity under the heavens." – Ecclesiastes 3:1

Personal Reflection Questions

1. Have you ever been in a season of waiting? How did you respond?

2. What is one area in your life where you need to trust God's timing?

3. How can you use your waiting time to grow closer to God?

Application: How to Trust God in the Waiting

1. Remember His Promises

Write down scriptures that remind you of God's faithfulness and read them daily.

2. Keep Serving and Growing

Use this season to grow in your faith, learn new skills, and serve others.

3. Stay Encouraged

Surround yourself with people who will encourage you and remind you of God's plan.

Study Guide: "Waiting on God"

Memory Verse: Ecclesiastes 3:1

"There is a time for everything, and a season for every activity under the heavens."

Daily Reading Plan:

- Day 1: Psalm 27:14 – Waiting on the Lord
- Day 2: 1 Samuel 16 – David's anointing but delayed kingship
- Day 3: Romans 5:3-5 – How suffering produces character
- Day 4: Habakkuk 2:3 – God's promises will come at the right time
- Day 5: Isaiah 40:31 – Renewing strength while waiting

Discussion Questions:

1. How do you feel when God asks you to wait?
2. What lessons have you learned in past waiting seasons?
3. How can you encourage someone else who is waiting on God?

Conclusion: Trust That God is Working

Waiting is never wasted. God is using every moment to prepare you for something greater. Trust Him, stay faithful, and remember—He's not through with you yet!

Fear often keeps us from trusting God's plan. In the next chapter, we will explore how to replace fear with faith and step into God's promises with confidence.

CHAPTER 4

Faith Over Fear

Fear is one of the biggest obstacles to fulfilling God's plan for our lives. It can paralyze us, make us doubt God's promises, and keep us from stepping into our destiny. However, the Bible teaches us that faith and fear cannot coexist—we must choose one.

In this chapter, we will explore how to overcome fear with faith, trust God's promises, and step boldly into what He has called us to do.

1. Fear Is Not from God

Fear is a tool of the enemy, meant to distract and discourage us from walking in faith. However, God has not given us a spirit of fear—He has given us power, love, and a sound mind.

Key Scripture:

"For God has not given us a spirit of fear, but of power and of love and of a sound mind." – 2 Timothy 1:7

Whenever fear tries to creep into your heart, remember that it does not come from God. Instead, He has equipped you with strength, love, and wisdom.

2. Examples of Faith Overcoming Fear in the Bible

2.1. Peter Walking on Water (Matthew 14:25-31)

Peter stepped out of the boat in faith, but as soon as he focused on the wind and waves, fear took over, and he began to sink. Jesus immediately reached out and saved him.

Lesson: When we keep our eyes on Jesus, faith sustains us. When we focus on our problems, fear takes over.

2.2. Joshua and Caleb vs. The Other Spies (Numbers 13-14)

When the Israelites sent 12 spies to explore the Promised Land, 10 came back fearful, saying the land was too dangerous. Only Joshua and Caleb had faith that God would give them victory.

Lesson: Fear will always try to make you doubt God's promises, but faith says, "If God said it, He will do it."

2.3. Gideon's Transformation (Judges 6-7)

Gideon started out afraid and doubting God's calling, but as he trusted God step by step, his faith grew, and he led an army to victory.

Lesson: Faith isn't about being fearless—it's about obeying God even when you feel afraid.

3. Faith Requires Action

Faith is not just believing—it's acting on what God has said, even when you don't see the full picture.

Key Scripture:

"Faith by itself, if it is not accompanied by action, is dead." – James 2:17

If we say we trust God but don't take steps of faith, we are not really trusting Him.

4. How to Strengthen Your Faith and Overcome Fear

4.1. Speak God's Word Over Your Life

Fear often begins in our thoughts. Replace fearful thoughts with God's truth.

Example: If you feel afraid, declare:

"I can do all things through Christ who strengthens me." – Philippians 4:13

4.2. Take Small Steps of Obedience

You don't have to have all the answers before stepping out in faith. Take the first step, and God will guide you.

Example: Abraham obeyed God without knowing exactly where he was going (Hebrews 11:8).

4.3. Pray for Courage

Ask God to increase your faith and remove fear from your heart.

Key Scripture:

"When I am afraid, I put my trust in you." – Psalm 56:3

Personal Reflection Questions

1. What is one area of your life where fear is holding you back?
2. How can you replace fear with faith in that area?

3. What is one step of faith you feel God is asking you to take?

Application: How to Walk in Faith Daily

1. Trust in God's Promises

Read and memorize scriptures that remind you of His faithfulness.

2. Surround Yourself with Faith-Filled People

Fear spreads easily, but so does faith. Be around people who encourage your faith.

3. Step Out, Even When It Feels Uncomfortable

Faith requires us to move forward, even when we feel unsure.

Study Guide: "Faith Over Fear"

Memory Verse: 2 Timothy 1:7

"For God has not given us a spirit of fear, but of power and of love and of a sound mind."

Daily Reading Plan:

- Day 1: Matthew 14:25-31 – Peter walks on water
- Day 2: Numbers 13-14 – Joshua and Caleb's faith
- Day 3: Judges 6-7 – Gideon's transformation
- Day 4: Hebrews 11:1-8 – The nature of faith
- Day 5: Psalm 56:3 – Trusting God when afraid

Discussion Questions:

    1.Can you think of a time when fear stopped you from doing something?

    2.What is one Bible verse that helps you overcome fear?

    3.How can you encourage others to walk in faith?

Conclusion: Choose Faith Over Fear

Fear will always try to stop you, but God is calling you to step out in faith. Trust Him, take action, and watch how He moves in your

Now that we've talked about faith, the next challenge is dealing with obstacles.

CHAPTER 5

Overcoming Obstacles

Every believer will face obstacles in life—difficulties, setbacks, opposition, and even spiritual warfare. But no obstacle is bigger than our God. He specializes in making a way where there seems to be no way.

In this chapter, we will learn how to overcome obstacles by relying on God's strength, standing firm in faith, and persevering through challenges.

1. Obstacles Are Part of the Process

Many people believe that if something is God's will, it should be easy. But throughout the Bible, we see that even when God calls us to something, we will face challenges along the way.

Example: The Israelites at the Red Sea (Exodus 14)

When God delivered the Israelites from Egypt, He led them to the Red Sea—with Pharaoh's army chasing behind them. It seemed like an impossible situation, but God parted the sea and made a way.

Key Lesson: Just because you face an obstacle doesn't mean you're on the wrong path. God allows challenges to show His power!

Key Scripture:

"The Lord will fight for you; you need only to be still." – Exodus 14:14

2. Obstacles Often Come Before Breakthrough

Before every major breakthrough, there is often a big challenge.

Example: The Walls of Jericho (Joshua 6)

God promised the Israelites victory in Jericho, but they first had to face huge, fortified walls. Instead of attacking in their own strength, they obeyed God's instructions—marching around the walls for seven days. On the seventh day, the walls fell down!

Key Lesson: God's strategy may not always make sense, but obedience leads to breakthrough.

Key Scripture:

"We walk by faith, not by sight." – 2 Corinthians 5:7

3. How to Overcome Obstacles God's Way

3.1. Trust God's Power, Not Your Own

When you face difficulties, don't rely on your own strength—rely on God.

Key Scripture:

"Not by might nor by power, but by My Spirit, says the Lord Almighty." – Zechariah 4:6

3.2. Stay Focused on God's Promises

Instead of focusing on how big the problem is, focus on how big God is.

Example: David and Goliath (1 Samuel 17) – David wasn't intimidated by the giant because he focused on God's power, not the size of his enemy.

Key Scripture:

"If God is for us, who can be against us?" – Romans 8:31

3.3. Speak Faith, Not Fear

Your words have power. Instead of speaking fear and doubt, declare God's promises.

Key Scripture:

"Death and life are in the power of the tongue." – Proverbs 18:21

4. When You Feel Stuck: Keep Moving Forward

Even when things seem impossible, don't quit. Take the next step in faith.

Example: The Woman with the Issue of Blood (Mark 5:25-34)

She had suffered for 12 years, but she didn't give up. She pressed through the crowd to touch Jesus' garment, and she was healed.

Key Lesson: If she had given up, she would have missed her miracle. Keep moving forward in faith!

Key Scripture:

"Let us run with endurance the race that is set before us, fixing our eyes on Jesus." – Hebrews 12:1-2

Personal Reflection Questions

1. What obstacles are you currently facing in your life?

2. Are you trusting God's power, or are you relying on your own strength?

3. What is one faith-filled step you can take this week to move forward?

Application: How to Overcome Obstacles Daily

1. Pray for Strength and Wisdom

Ask God for the strength to endure and the wisdom to navigate challenges.

2. Stand on His Promises

Write down Bible verses that encourage you and read them daily.

3. Take Action in Faith

Even when you don't see the full picture, keep obeying God and moving forward.

Study Guide: "Overcoming Obstacles"

Memory Verse: Exodus 14:14

"The Lord will fight for you; you need only to be still."

Daily Reading Plan:

- Day 1: Exodus 14 – The Red Sea miracle
- Day 2: Joshua 6 – The walls of Jericho
- Day 3: 1 Samuel 17 – David and Goliath
- Day 4: Mark 5:25-34 – The woman with the issue of blood
- Day 5: 2 Corinthians 5:7 – Walking by faith, not by sight

Discussion Questions:

1. Have you ever faced an obstacle that later led to a breakthrough?

2. How can you encourage someone who is struggling with challenges?

3. What is one thing you can do today to overcome a current obstacle?

Conclusion: No Obstacle is Bigger Than God

Obstacles are part of life, but they are not the end of the story. With God's help, you can overcome anything. Keep trusting, keep believing, and keep moving forward!

Now that we've learned how to overcome obstacles, we will discuss spiritual warfare—understanding the battles we face and how to fight in the Spirit.

CHAPTER 6

Spiritual Warfare

Fighting the Right Battles

As believers, we are in a spiritual battle every day. The enemy does not want us to walk in God's purpose, so he attacks our faith, our minds, and our relationships. But the good news is God has given us the weapons to win!

In this chapter, we will learn how to recognize spiritual warfare, how to fight the right battles, and how to use the armor of God to stand firm in victory.

1. Recognizing Spiritual Warfare

Not every struggle is physical or emotional—some battles are spiritual. The enemy tries to attack us in subtle ways so we don't even realize we're in a fight.

Key Scripture:

"For we wrestle not against flesh and blood, but against principalities, against powers, against the rulers of the darkness of this world, against spiritual wickedness in high places." – Ephesians 6:12

Common Signs of Spiritual Warfare:

- Unusual struggles in your faith (doubts, discouragement, feeling distant from God)
- Constant negative thoughts (fear, anxiety, condemnation)

- Attacks on your relationships (division, conflict, misunderstandings)
- Unexplainable resistance (every time you try to grow in God, something tries to stop you)

Example: When Daniel prayed, his answer was delayed for 21 days because of spiritual opposition (Daniel 10:12-13). Sometimes, delays are spiritual battles.

2. Fighting the Right Battles

Many people waste their energy fighting the wrong battles—arguing with people, trying to fix everything in their own strength, or getting distracted by small things. But the real battle is in the spiritual realm.

Key Scripture:

"The weapons we fight with are not the weapons of the world. On the contrary, they have divine power to demolish strongholds." – 2 Corinthians 10:4

3. Wrong Ways to Fight:

1. Fighting with people (Ephesians 6:12 – people are not the real enemy)

2. Fighting in your own strength (Zechariah 4:6 – victory comes by God's Spirit)

3. Fighting without prayer (James 5:16 – prayer is our greatest weapon)

4. The Armor of God – How to Win Spiritual Battles

Ephesians 6:10-18 tells us to put on the full armor of God to stand against the enemy. Let's break it down:

3.1. The Belt of Truth

Truth holds everything together. The enemy tries to defeat us with lies, but we must stand on God's truth.

Key Scripture: "Sanctify them by the truth; Your word is truth." – John 17:17

3.2. The Breastplate of Righteousness

Righteousness protects our hearts. When we live in obedience to God, we guard ourselves from the enemy's attacks.

Key Scripture: "Guard your heart above all else, for it determines the course of your life." – Proverbs 4:23

3.3. The Shoes of the Gospel of Peace

We must stand firm in God's peace no matter what happens around us.

Key Scripture: "And the peace of God, which surpasses all understanding, will guard your hearts and your minds in Christ Jesus." – Philippians 4:7

3.4. The Shield of Faith

Faith protects us from the enemy's attacks—doubt, fear, and worry.

Key Scripture: "For we live by faith, not by sight." – 2 Corinthians 5:7

3.5. The Helmet of Salvation

The helmet protects our minds from lies and confusion.

Key Scripture: "Take every thought captive to obey Christ." – 2 Corinthians 10:5

3.6. The Sword of the Spirit (God's Word)

God's Word is our weapon to defeat the enemy.

Example: When Jesus was tempted in the wilderness, He used scripture to fight back (Matthew 4:1-11).

Key Scripture: "The Word of God is alive and powerful, sharper than any two-edged sword." – Hebrews 4:12

4. How to Fight and Win

4.1. Stay Close to God

Your relationship with God is your greatest defense.

Key Scripture: "Draw near to God, and He will draw near to you." – James 4:8

4.2. Pray with Authority

Prayer is not just asking—it's a weapon. Speak God's Word boldly!

Key Scripture: "Resist the devil, and he will flee from you." – James 4:7

4.3. Declare Victory in Faith

Even when things look bad, declare God's promises over your life.

Example: The Israelites shouted before the walls of Jericho fell (Joshua 6).

Key Scripture: "We are more than conquerors through Him who loved us." – Romans 8:37

Personal Reflection Questions

1. Have you recognized any spiritual battles in your life?

2. Are you using the armor of God daily?

3. What changes can you make to strengthen your spiritual defenses?

Application: How to Stand Strong in Spiritual Warfare

1. Pray Daily for Protection

Ask God to cover you with His armor every morning.

2. Read and Speak Scripture

The Word of God is your greatest weapon.

3. Be Aware of the Enemy's Tactics

Recognize when struggles are spiritual attacks, and fight back with prayer.

Study Guide: "Spiritual Warfare"

Memory Verse: Ephesians 6:12

"For we wrestle not against flesh and blood, but against principalities, against powers, against the rulers of the darkness of this world, against spiritual wickedness in high places."

Daily Reading Plan:

- Day 1: Ephesians 6:10-18 – The Armor of God
- Day 2: 2 Corinthians 10:3-5 – Our weapons are not worldly
- Day 3: Daniel 10:12-13 – Delays in prayer are sometimes spiritual warfare
- Day 4: Matthew 4:1-11 – Jesus resists the devil using scripture
- Day 5: James 4:7 – Resist the devil, and he will flee

Discussion Questions:

1. How can you tell when you are in a spiritual battle?

2. Which part of the armor of God do you need to focus on the most?

3. How can you encourage someone else in their spiritual battles?

Conclusion: The Victory is Already Won!

The enemy may attack, but Jesus has already won the battle! As believers, we fight from victory, not for victory. Stay strong, use your spiritual weapons, and walk in the power of God!

Now that we understand spiritual warfare, we will dive into prayer—the most powerful weapon in the life of a believer.

CHAPTER 7

The Power of Prayer

Prayer is one of the most powerful tools that God has given us. It is not just a religious ritual—it is a direct line of communication with God. Through prayer, we can receive guidance, strength, healing, and breakthrough. Yet, many believers struggle with prayer because they don't realize its power or don't know how to use it effectively.

In this chapter, we will explore why prayer is essential, how Jesus taught us to pray, and how to develop a powerful and effective prayer life.

1. Why Prayer is Powerful

Prayer is not just about asking God for things—it is about building a relationship with Him.

Key Scripture:

"The prayer of a righteous person is powerful and effective." – James 5:16

God hears and responds to the prayers of His people. Prayer invites God into our situation, aligns us with His will, and releases His power into our lives.

2. Jesus' Example: How He Prayed

Jesus had a powerful prayer life, and He showed us how important prayer is.

2.1. Jesus Prayed Regularly

•He often withdrew to pray alone (Luke 5:16).

- He prayed early in the morning (Mark 1:35).

- He prayed before making big decisions (Luke 6:12-13).

Lesson: If Jesus needed to pray, how much more do we?

2.2. Jesus Taught His Disciples to Pray

The disciples asked Jesus, "Lord, teach us to pray." (Luke 11:1)

He gave them what we call The Lord's Prayer, which serves as a model for us.

3. The Lord's Prayer: A Guide to Effective Prayer

In Matthew 6:9-13, Jesus gave us a structure for prayer. Let's break it down:

3.1. "Our Father in Heaven, Hallowed Be Your Name"

- Begin with worship and reverence for God.

- Recognize who He is—our loving Father.

3.2. "Your Kingdom Come, Your Will Be Done"

- Surrender your plans and desires to God's will.

- Pray for His kingdom to be established in your life.

3.3. "Give Us This Day Our Daily Bread"

- Ask for God's provision—spiritually and physically.

- Trust Him to meet your needs each day.

3.4. "Forgive Us Our Sins, As We Forgive Others"

- Confess your sins and ask for forgiveness.
- Forgive those who have hurt you.

3.5. "Lead Us Not Into Temptation, But Deliver Us From Evil"

- Ask for strength to resist temptation.
- Pray for protection against spiritual attacks.

4. The Power of Persistent Prayer

Sometimes, answers to prayer don't come immediately. Persistent prayer is key.

Example: The Persistent Widow (Luke 18:1-8)

Jesus told a parable about a widow who kept asking a judge for justice. Because she kept asking, he finally granted her request.

Lesson: Keep praying—even when you don't see results right away.

Key Scripture:

"Ask, and it will be given to you; seek, and you will find; knock, and the door will be opened to you." – Matthew 7:7

5. Different Types of Prayer

Prayer comes in many forms. Here are a few:

5.1. Prayer of Adoration (Worship)

- Praising God for who He is.

•Example: "Bless the Lord, O my soul, and forget not all His benefits." – Psalm 103:2

5.2. Prayer of Confession

•Admitting our sins and asking for forgiveness.

•Example: "If we confess our sins, He is faithful and just to forgive us." – 1 John 1:9

5.3. Prayer of Thanksgiving

•Thanking God for His blessings.

•Example: "Give thanks in all circumstances." – 1 Thessalonians 5:18

5.4. Prayer of Supplication (Asking for Needs)

•Bringing our requests to God.

•Example: "Do not be anxious about anything, but in every situation, by prayer and petition, with thanksgiving, present your requests to God." – Philippians 4:6

5.5. Intercessory Prayer (Praying for Others)

•Praying for family, friends, and the world.

•Example: Jesus prayed for Peter's faith (Luke 22:31-32).

6. How to Build a Strong Prayer Life

6.1. Set a Regular Prayer Time

•Make prayer a daily habit (morning, night, or throughout the day).

6.2. Pray with Faith

•Believe that God hears you.

•Key Scripture: "Without faith, it is impossible to please God." – Hebrews 11:6

6.3. Pray the Word of God

•Use Bible verses in your prayers—it strengthens your faith.

6.4. Keep a Prayer Journal

•Write down your prayers and record answered prayers.

Personal Reflection Questions

1. How often do you pray, and what could help you improve your prayer life?

2. Which part of The Lord's Prayer speaks to you the most?

3. What is one thing you can start praying for persistently?

Application: How to Strengthen Your Prayer Life Daily

1. Set a Prayer Goal

Decide on a specific time each day to spend in prayer.

2. Use a Prayer List

Write down the people and situations you want to pray for regularly.

3. Pray with Others

Join a prayer group or find a prayer partner to encourage you.

Study Guide: "The Power of Prayer"

Memory Verse: James 5:16

"The prayer of a righteous person is powerful and effective."

Daily Reading Plan:

- •Day 1: Matthew 6:9-13 – The Lord's Prayer
- •Day 2: Luke 18:1-8 – The Persistent Widow
- •Day 3: Philippians 4:6-7 – Pray with thanksgiving
- •Day 4: 1 Thessalonians 5:16-18 – Pray without ceasing
- •Day 5: James 5:16 – The power of prayer

Discussion Questions:

1. What obstacles keep people from praying regularly?

2. How can you make prayer a greater priority in your life?

3. What is one prayer request you have seen God answer?

Conclusion: Prayer Changes Everything

Prayer is not a last resort—it should be our first response. When we pray, we connect with God, release His power, and align ourselves with His will. Keep praying, keep believing, and watch God move in your life!

Now that we've talked about prayer, the next step is obedience—because hearing from God means nothing if we don't do what He says!

CHAPTER 8

Walking In Obedience

Obedience to God is the key to living a victorious Christian life. Many people want to experience God's blessings, power, and guidance, but they struggle with fully surrendering to His will. Obedience is more than just following rules—it is an act of love and trust.

In this chapter, we will explore why obedience is important, how it brings blessings, and how to develop a heart that is quick to obey God.

1. Why Obedience Matters

Many people say they love God, but true love is shown through obedience. Jesus made it clear:

Key Scripture:

"If you love Me, keep My commandments." – John 14:15

Obedience is not about following a list of rules—it is about a relationship with God. When we obey, we show that we trust Him and believe His ways are best.

2. The Blessings of Obedience

When we walk in obedience, we unlock God's blessings in our lives.

2.1. Obedience Brings Favor

God blesses those who walk in His ways.

Example: Abraham obeyed God, even when asked to leave his homeland (Genesis 12:1-4). Because of his obedience, God made him the father of many nations.

Key Scripture:

"Blessed are all who fear the Lord, who walk in obedience to Him." – Psalm 128:1

2.2. Obedience Brings Protection

When we obey God, we stay under His divine protection.

Example: Noah obeyed God and built the ark, even when it didn't make sense. His obedience saved his family from the flood (Genesis 6:22).

Key Scripture:

"The Lord watches over the way of the righteous, but the way of the wicked leads to destruction." – Psalm 1:6

2.3. Obedience Leads to Spiritual Growth

The more we obey, the more we grow in our faith.

Example: The disciples followed Jesus' instructions, even when they didn't fully understand. Because of their obedience, they experienced miracles and deepened their faith.

Key Scripture:

"But be doers of the word, and not hearers only, deceiving yourselves." – James 1:22

3. Partial Obedience is Still Disobedience

Sometimes, we obey God halfway but still expect full blessings. However, partial obedience is disobedience in God's eyes.

Example: King Saul's Disobedience (1 Samuel 15)

- God told Saul to destroy everything from the Amalekites.
- Instead, he kept some things for himself.
- As a result, God rejected him as king.

Lesson: We can't pick and choose what parts of God's instructions we want to follow.

Key Scripture:

"To obey is better than sacrifice, and to heed is better than the fat of rams." – 1 Samuel 15:22

4. Overcoming the Struggle to Obey

We all struggle with obedience sometimes. Here's how to overcome it:

4.1. Trust God's Plan

- Sometimes, we don't understand why God asks us to do something.
- Trust that He sees the bigger picture.

Key Scripture:

"Trust in the Lord with all your heart and lean not on your own understanding." – Proverbs 3:5

4.2. Let Go of Fear

- Fear of the unknown keeps many people from obeying God.
- But God never calls us to something without providing for us.

Example: Peter obeyed Jesus and stepped out of the boat in faith (Matthew 14:28-29).

Key Scripture:

"For God has not given us a spirit of fear, but of power, love, and a sound mind." – 2 Timothy 1:7

4.3. Surrender Your Will

- Jesus is our greatest example of obedience.
- Before going to the cross, He prayed, "Not my will, but Yours be done." (Luke 22:42)

Lesson: True obedience requires surrendering our own desires to God's will.

Personal Reflection Questions

1. Is there an area in your life where you struggle with obedience?

2. Have you ever experienced the blessings of obedience?

3. What steps can you take to trust God more fully?

Application: How to Walk in Obedience Daily

1. Read and Follow God's Word

   •The Bible is our instruction manual for life.

2. Listen to the Holy Spirit

   •The Holy Spirit will guide you in your daily decisions.

3. Obey Even When It's Hard

   •Trust that God's ways are always best.

Study Guide: "Walking in Obedience"

Memory Verse: John 14:15

"If you love Me, keep My commandments."

Daily Reading Plan:

   •Day 1: Genesis 12:1-4 – Abraham's obedience

   •Day 2: 1 Samuel 15 – Saul's disobedience

   •Day 3: Luke 5:1-11 – The disciples obey Jesus

   •Day 4: Proverbs 3:5-6 – Trusting God's plan

   •Day 5: James 1:22 – Being doers of the Word

Discussion Questions:

1. What are some excuses people use to avoid obeying God?

2. How can we strengthen our trust in God's instructions?

3. What is one step of obedience you can take this week?

Conclusion: Obedience Leads to Blessings

Walking in obedience is not always easy, but it is always worth it. God rewards those who follow Him with favor, protection, and spiritual growth. No matter what He asks of you, trust Him and obey—because He's not through with you yet!

Now that we understand obedience, we will explore how God tests our faith to make us stronger.

CHAPTER 9

The Testing Of Your Faith

As a believer, you will encounter times when your faith is to the test. These tests can be uncomfortable, but they are not meant to break you; rather, they are designed to strengthen you. In this chapter, we will look at why God allows our faith to be tested, the purpose behind these trials, and how we can respond to them with courage and trust.

1. Why Does God Test Our Faith?

Many people wonder why God allows trials and challenges in their lives. The truth is that faith is refined through testing. God uses these tests to purify us and help us grow into the people He has called us to be.

Key Scripture:

"These have come so that the proven genuineness of your faith—of greater worth than gold, which perishes even though refined by fire—may result in praise, glory, and honor when Jesus Christ is revealed." – 1 Peter 1:7

Just like gold is purified by fire, our faith is strengthened by the trials we face. God is not punishing us; He is refining us for greater purposes.

2. The Purpose of Testing

Faith tests serve several important purposes:

2.1. To Strengthen Our Faith

When our faith is tested, we discover whether it is genuine or merely based on circumstances. Testing purifies and strengthens us.

Example: Abraham's faith was tested when God asked him to sacrifice his son, Isaac. His willingness to obey demonstrated his unwavering trust in God (Genesis 22:1-19).

Key Scripture:

"Consider it pure joy, my brothers and sisters, whenever you face trials of many kinds, because you know that the testing of your faith produces perseverance." – James 1:2-3

2.2. To Build Our Character

God uses tests to shape our character. Trials help develop virtues like patience, endurance, and humility.

Example: Job's faith was tested through intense suffering. Despite losing everything, he declared, "Though He slay me, yet will I trust in Him" (Job 13:15). Through his testing, Job's character was refined.

Key Scripture:

"We also glory in our sufferings, because we know that suffering produces perseverance; perseverance, character; and character, hope." – Romans 5:3-4

2.3. To Bring Us Closer to God

Sometimes God allows tests to draw us nearer to Himself. In moments of struggle, we seek His presence more urgently, and this deepens our relationship with Him.

Example: The Israelites experienced hardship in the wilderness, but during that time, God revealed His faithfulness and provision to them (Exodus 16:4-36).

Key Scripture:

"Draw near to God, and He will draw near to you." – James 4:8

3. Types of Faith Tests

There are different types of faith tests, and each one serves a specific purpose.

3.1. The Test of Patience

This is when you have to wait for God's timing. It can be difficult, but patience teaches us to trust God's plan.

Example: Joseph had to wait many years after receiving a promise from God before he saw the fulfillment of that promise (Genesis 37, 41).

Key Scripture:

"But if we hope for what we do not yet have, we wait for it patiently." – Romans 8:25

3.2. The Test of Trust

Sometimes God asks us to trust Him even when we don't understand the situation. Trusting God with our lives and decisions requires a deep level of surrender.

Example: When God called Moses to confront Pharaoh, Moses didn't know how Pharaoh would react, but he trusted God to deliver the Israelites from slavery (Exodus 3:10-12).

Key Scripture:

"Trust in the Lord with all your heart and lean not on your own understanding." – Proverbs 3:5

3.3. The Test of Obedience

As we discussed in the previous chapter, God often tests our obedience. He asks us to obey His Word, even when it doesn't make sense, because obedience leads to blessings.

Example: Jesus Himself faced the ultimate test of obedience in the Garden of Gethsemane, where He prayed, "Not my will, but Yours be done" (Luke 22:42).

Key Scripture:

"If you love me, keep my commandments." – John 14:15

4. How to Pass the Test

Faith tests may seem overwhelming, but God equips us to face them. Here's how we can approach these tests with faith:

4.1. Stay Rooted in God's Word

The Bible is our foundation during times of testing. The promises of God give us hope and remind us of His faithfulness.

Key Scripture:

"I have hidden your word in my heart that I might not sin against you." – Psalm 119:11

4.2. Pray for Strength

Prayer is essential when facing trials. God gives us the strength to endure and helps us see things from His perspective.

Key Scripture:

"I can do all this through Him who gives me strength." – Philippians 4:13

4.3. Remember God's Faithfulness

In times of testing, it's easy to forget how faithful God has been in the past. Remind yourself of the ways He has come through for you.

Key Scripture:

"Remember the wonders He has done, His miracles, and the judgments He pronounced." – Psalm 105:5

4.4. Keep a Positive Attitude

Trials can be discouraging, but maintaining a positive, grateful attitude can help you endure.

Key Scripture:

"Rejoice in the Lord always. I will say it again: Rejoice!" – Philippians 4:4

Personal Reflection Questions

1. What has been one of the greatest tests of your faith, and how did you respond?

2. How do you typically react when your faith is tested?

3. What can you do to strengthen your trust in God during difficult times?

Application: Embracing Your Faith Tests

1. View Trials as Opportunities for Growth

Instead of seeing tests as obstacles, view them as opportunities for spiritual growth. Every trial is a chance to become more like Christ.

2. Prepare for the Next Test

Stay grounded in God's Word and continue to seek His presence, so when the next trial comes, you are ready to face it with faith and strength.

Study Guide: "The Testing of Your Faith"

Memory Verse: James 1:3

"Because you know that the testing of your faith produces perseverance."

Daily Reading Plan:

- Day 1: 1 Peter 1:6-7 – The testing of faith
- Day 2: Job 1 – Job's trials
- Day 3: Genesis 22 – Abraham's obedience
- Day 4: Romans 5:3-4 – The benefits of suffering
- Day 5: Philippians 4:4-7 – Joy in the Lord during trials

Discussion Questions:

1. How does knowing that God is refining your faith change your perspective on trials?

2. What steps can you take to remain faithful when faced with difficult circumstances?

3. How can you encourage others who are struggling with their faith?

Conclusion: Faith Tested, Faith Strengthened

The testing of your faith is an inevitable part of the Christian journey, but it's not something to fear. Remember, God is using it to refine and strengthen you. As you persevere through these trials, you will emerge more mature, more trusting, and more equipped to fulfill God's purposes for your life.

In the next chapter, we will explore how to trust God when life feels like a storm. When the winds of adversity blow, how can we remain steadfast in our faith?

CHAPTER 10

Trusting God In The Storm

Life is full of storms—trials, challenges, and uncertainties that can shake us to the core. Whether it's a personal crisis, a health issue, or a financial struggle, it's easy to feel overwhelmed by the storms of life. In this chapter, we will explore how to trust God in the midst of these storms. Just as Jesus calmed the storm for His disciples, He offers us peace and stability, no matter how fierce the storms may be.

1. Understanding Life's Storms

Storms are an inevitable part of life. No one is exempt from difficulties, but the way we respond can make all the difference. Jesus Himself warned us that we would face challenges in this world, but He also promised that He would be with us through them.

Key Scripture:

"In this world, you will have trouble. But take heart! I have overcome the world." – John 16:33

The storms of life can be physical, emotional, or spiritual. Whatever form they take, they can challenge our faith and cause us to question God's goodness. Yet, these trials are not without purpose—they are opportunities for us to grow in trust and dependence on God.

2. The Storm on the Sea

One of the most well-known stories of Jesus calming a storm is found in the Gospels. The disciples were in a boat when a violent storm arose, and Jesus was asleep. They were afraid and woke Him, and He calmed the storm with just a word.

Key Scripture:

"He got up, rebuked the wind and the waves, and it was completely calm. Why are you so afraid? Do you still have no faith?" – Mark 4:39-40

This story is a powerful reminder that Jesus is in control, even when it feels like the storm is too powerful to handle. In the midst of the storm, we can trust that Jesus is with us, and He has the power to bring peace to our hearts.

3. Why Trusting God in the Storm Matters

When we choose to trust God in the midst of a storm, we are making a powerful statement about our faith. Trusting God does not mean ignoring our fears or pretending that the storm isn't real—it means choosing to believe that God is bigger than the storm.

3.1. Trusting God Deepens Our Relationship with Him

During storms, we often feel helpless and vulnerable. It is in these moments that we are most likely to turn to God for help. These times of dependence on Him strengthen our relationship and remind us of His faithfulness.

Example: King David often found himself in situations of distress, but he wrote songs of trust and reliance on God in his darkest moments (Psalm 23:1-4, Psalm 34:17-18).

3.2. Trusting God Demonstrates Our Faith

When we trust God in the storm, we are demonstrating our belief that He is sovereign and that He will provide for us, even when circumstances seem bleak.

Example: Shadrach, Meshach, and Abednego trusted God even when they were threatened with being thrown into a fiery furnace (Daniel 3:16-18). They knew that God was able to save them, but even if He chose not to, they would not bow to the king's idols.

Key Scripture:

"Though He slay me, yet will I trust in Him." – Job 13:15

4. How to Trust God in the Storm

Trusting God during storms is not always easy, but it is possible. Here are some practical steps to help you trust God during difficult times:

4.1. Focus on God's Character

When we face storms, we often focus on the problem. However, in those moments, we need to shift our focus to God's character. God is faithful, loving, and all-powerful. He is good, and He will never leave or forsake us.

Key Scripture:

"The Lord is close to the brokenhearted and saves those who are crushed in spirit." – Psalm 34:18

4.2. Remember God's Promises

The Bible is full of promises that remind us of God's love and care. In times of uncertainty, remind yourself of God's faithfulness and the promises He has made.

Key Scripture:

"Cast all your anxiety on Him because He cares for you." – 1 Peter 5:7

4.3. Pray and Surrender Your Worries

Instead of trying to control the storm, surrender your worries to God in prayer. Prayer is a powerful way to release our anxiety and trust in God's plan.

Key Scripture:

"Do not be anxious about anything, but in every situation, by prayer and petition, with thanksgiving, present your requests to God." – Philippians 4:6

4.4. Praise God in the Storm

It may seem difficult, but praising God in the storm is an act of faith. When we choose to worship in the midst of our struggles, we declare that God is worthy, regardless of our circumstances.

Example: Paul and Silas were in prison, but they prayed and sang hymns to God (Acts 16:25). Their faith in the midst of trial led to a miraculous deliverance.

Key Scripture:

"Rejoice in the Lord always. I will say it again: Rejoice!" – Philippians 4:4

5. The Storm Will Pass

No storm lasts forever. The difficulties we face in life are temporary, and God has a purpose for them. Trusting Him in the storm will bring us closer to Him and help us emerge stronger in our faith.

Example: Jesus calmed the storm for His disciples, and when the storm passed, they were amazed by His power (Mark 4:41). The storm didn't last, but the lesson they learned about trusting Jesus remained with them.

Key Scripture:

"For our light and momentary troubles are achieving for us an eternal glory that far outweighs them all." – 2 Corinthians 4:17

Personal Reflection Questions

1. What storms are you currently facing in your life?

2. How can you shift your focus from the storm to God's character and promises?

3. In what ways can you praise God in the midst of your difficulties?

Application: Trusting God in the Midst of Life's Storms

1. Seek God's Presence

In the midst of your storm, make time to spend in God's presence through prayer and worship. Seek His comfort and strength.

2. Encourage Others to Trust God

When you are walking through a storm, look for opportunities to encourage others who are facing similar struggles. Your testimony of God's faithfulness can bring hope to others.

Study Guide: "Trusting God in the Storm"

Memory Verse: Philippians 4:6

"Do not be anxious about anything, but in every situation, by prayer and petition, with thanksgiving, present your requests to God."

Daily Reading Plan:

- Day 1: Mark 4:35-41 – Jesus calms the storm
- Day 2: Psalm 23:1-4 – Trusting in God's guidance
- Day 3: 2 Corinthians 4:7-18 – Hope in the midst of trials
- Day 4: Isaiah 41:10 – God's promises of support
- Day 5: Acts 16:25-34 – Praising God in difficult circumstances

Discussion Questions:

1. How do you respond to storms in your life?

2. What are some specific promises of God that you can hold on to during difficult times?

3. How can you cultivate a heart of praise even in challenging circumstances?

Conclusion: Peace in the Midst of the Storm

Though the storms of life can feel overwhelming, remember that God is always with us. We can trust in His power, His character, and His promises. Just as Jesus calmed the storm on the sea, He offers us peace in the midst of our trials. Keep trusting, keep praying, and keep praising, because He is with you through every storm.

In the next chapter, we will explore the life-changing power of forgiveness—how it heals us, frees us, and enables us to walk in God's peace.

CHAPTER 11

The Power of Forgiveness

Forgiveness is one of the most powerful and transformative principles in the Christian faith. It has the power to heal broken relationships, set us free from bitterness, and restore peace to our hearts. But forgiveness isn't always easy. Sometimes, we hold onto the pain of past offenses, and letting go feels impossible. In this chapter, we will explore the power of forgiveness—why it's essential for our spiritual growth, how we can forgive others, and the incredible freedom that comes from forgiving.

1. The Command to Forgive

As followers of Christ, we are commanded to forgive others, just as God has forgiven us. Forgiveness is not optional; it is a foundational principle of the Christian life. Jesus made it clear that our willingness to forgive others is directly tied to our own forgiveness from God.

Key Scripture:

"And forgive us our debts, as we also have forgiven our debtors." – Matthew 6:12

In the Lord's Prayer, Jesus instructs us to ask God for forgiveness, but He also reminds us that we must forgive those who have wronged us.

Key Scripture:

"For if you forgive other people when they sin against you, your heavenly Father will also forgive you. But if you do not forgive others their sins, your Father will not forgive your sins." – Matthew 6:14-15

Jesus is clear: forgiveness is not optional for believers. Our ability to forgive others is a reflection of the grace that we have received from God.

2. Why Forgiveness Is Essential

2.1. Forgiveness Restores Our Relationship with God

When we hold onto unforgiveness, it creates a barrier between us and God. Sinful attitudes, such as bitterness, resentment, and hatred, hinder our fellowship with Him. By forgiving others, we remove that barrier and restore intimacy with God.

Example: In the parable of the unforgiving servant (Matthew 18:21-35), Jesus teaches that when we fail to forgive others, it reflects a lack of understanding of the grace God has shown us.

2.2. Forgiveness Sets Us Free

Unforgiveness keeps us trapped in the past. When we refuse to forgive, we allow the offense to control our emotions, thoughts, and even our actions. Forgiveness frees us from the power of that hurt and enables us to move forward with peace.

Key Scripture:

"Get rid of all bitterness, rage and anger, brawling and slander, along with every form of malice. Be kind and compassionate to one another, forgiving each other, just as in Christ God forgave you." – Ephesians 4:31-32

2.3. Forgiveness Restores Relationships

Forgiveness is essential for healing broken relationships. When we forgive, we make a choice to let go of past offenses and create space for reconciliation and restoration. Forgiveness does not mean that we condone the wrong, but that we release the person from the debt they owe us.

Example: Joseph's forgiveness of his brothers (Genesis 45:1-15) demonstrates how forgiving others can lead to healing and restoration, even in the most difficult circumstances.

3. How to Forgive

Forgiveness is not always easy, especially when the offense is deep or the hurt is ongoing. However, God gives us the grace to forgive, even in the most challenging situations. Here are some steps to help you forgive others:

3.1. Acknowledge the Hurt

Before you can forgive, you must first acknowledge the hurt. Denying or ignoring the pain only delays healing. Take time to process your emotions and recognize the offense for what it is.

Example: In the Psalms, David often expressed his pain to God (Psalm 34:18). God hears our hurt and is close to the brokenhearted.

Key Scripture:

"The Lord is close to the brokenhearted and saves those who are crushed in spirit." – Psalm 34:18

3.2. Choose to Forgive

Forgiveness is a choice, not a feeling. It may take time to heal emotionally, but the decision to forgive is made in the heart. When you choose to forgive, you are releasing the person from the debt they owe you and entrusting the situation to God.

Key Scripture:

"Forgive as the Lord forgave you." – Colossians 3:13

3.3. Pray for the Offender

Praying for the person who hurt you is one of the most powerful ways to release them. As you pray, ask God to bless them and work in their life. This doesn't mean that you condone their actions, but it helps you to soften your heart and trust God to deal with the situation.

Key Scripture:

"But I tell you, love your enemies and pray for those who persecute you." – Matthew 5:44

3.4. Let Go of the Right to Revenge

Forgiveness means letting go of the desire for revenge or justice. It's trusting that God is the ultimate Judge, and He will handle the situation in His way and His timing.

Key Scripture:

"Do not take revenge, my dear friends, but leave room for God's wrath, for it is written: 'It is mine to avenge; I will repay,' says the Lord." – Romans 12:19

4. The Benefits of Forgiveness

Forgiveness brings numerous benefits to our lives, both spiritually and emotionally:

4.1. Healing and Restoration

Forgiving others leads to healing. Holding onto unforgiveness often results in bitterness, resentment, and even physical stress. When we forgive, we open the door for emotional healing and peace.

Key Scripture:

"A heart at peace gives life to the body, but envy rots the bones." – Proverbs 14:30

4.2. Freedom from Bitterness

Forgiveness frees us from the prison of bitterness. Holding onto bitterness can consume us, but when we forgive, we release that bitterness and experience the freedom of a peaceful heart.

Key Scripture:

"Let all bitterness and wrath and anger and clamor and slander be put away from you, along with all malice." – Ephesians 4:31

4.3. Spiritual Growth

Choosing to forgive leads to spiritual maturity. It forces us to rely on God's strength and mercy, which helps us grow in compassion, humility, and grace.

Key Scripture:

"Be kind to one another, tenderhearted, forgiving one another, as God in Christ forgave you." – Ephesians 4:32

Personal Reflection Questions

1. Who do you need to forgive in your life?

2. How has unforgiveness affected your relationship with God and others?

3. What steps can you take today to begin the process of forgiveness?

Application: Living a Life of Forgiveness

1. Be Willing to Forgive Quickly

Don't let bitterness take root. Choose to forgive quickly, even in small offenses, so that your heart remains pure and free from anger.

2. Practice Forgiveness Regularly

Forgiveness is a continual process. Make a habit of forgiving others as Christ has forgiven you. It's a lifestyle that leads to peace and freedom.

Study Guide: "The Power of Forgiveness"

Memory Verse: Matthew 6:14-15

"For if you forgive other people when they sin against you, your heavenly Father will also forgive you."

Daily Reading Plan:

- Day 1: Matthew 18:21-35 – The parable of the unforgiving servant
- Day 2: Ephesians 4:31-32 – The call to forgive
- Day 3: Colossians 3:12-14 – Forgiveness and compassion
- Day 4: Matthew 5:43-48 – Loving and forgiving our enemies
- Day 5: Genesis 45:1-15 – Joseph forgives his brothers

Discussion Questions:

1. Why is it so difficult to forgive others, and how can we overcome this difficulty?

2. How has God's forgiveness of you affected your ability to forgive others?

3. What are some practical ways you can demonstrate forgiveness in your relationships?

Conclusion: Forgiveness as Freedom

Forgiveness is a powerful gift that not only heals relationships but also sets us free from the burden of bitterness and anger. When we forgive others, we reflect the incredible grace that God has shown us. Forgiveness is not a one-time act—it's a lifestyle of extending grace, mercy, and love to others as God has done for us.

In the next chapter, we will discuss how to experience and walk in the peace of God, even in the midst of life's challenges and struggles.

CHAPTER 12

Walking in God's Peace

In a world filled with chaos, anxiety, and uncertainty, it can often feel like peace is out of reach. Yet, as believers, we are promised the peace of God—a peace that surpasses understanding and guards our hearts and minds in Christ Jesus. This chapter explores what it means to walk in God's peace, how we can experience it daily, and how it transforms our lives.

1. The Promise of God's Peace

Jesus promised us peace, but not the kind of peace the world offers. The world's peace is often temporary and based on external circumstances, but the peace of God is lasting, unshakable, and rooted in His presence.

Key Scripture:

"Peace I leave with you; my peace I give you. I do not give to you as the world gives. Do not let your hearts be troubled and do not be afraid." – John 14:27

In this verse, Jesus reassures His disciples that His peace is different—it's not based on circumstances, but on His unchanging love and sovereignty. This peace is available to us, no matter what we face.

2. The Source of God's Peace

The peace of God comes from knowing Him personally and trusting in His sovereignty. It's rooted in a relationship with

God, not in our ability to control our circumstances. When we focus on God and His promises, we can experience His peace, even in the midst of difficult situations.

2.1. Peace through Trusting God

One of the key ways to experience God's peace is by trusting in Him. Trusting that He is in control, that He loves us, and that He works all things together for our good (Romans 8:28) brings peace to our hearts.

Key Scripture:

"You will keep in perfect peace those whose minds are steadfast because they trust in you." – Isaiah 26:3

The more we trust in God, the more His peace will guard our hearts. Trust is the foundation of peace.

2.2. Peace through Prayer

Prayer is another powerful way to access God's peace. When we present our requests to God with thanksgiving, He promises to give us peace that surpasses understanding.

Key Scripture:

"Do not be anxious about anything, but in every situation, by prayer and petition, with thanksgiving, present your requests to God. And the peace of God, which transcends all understanding, will guard your hearts and your minds in Christ Jesus." – Philippians 4:6-7

Prayer shifts our focus from our worries to God's faithfulness. As we cast our anxieties on Him, we experience His peace.

3. Walking in God's Peace Daily

Walking in God's peace is not a one-time experience—it is a daily decision to rely on His presence and promises. Here are some practical steps to help you walk in His peace:

3.1. Set Your Mind on Things Above

To experience God's peace, we must fix our minds on eternal truths, not on the temporary troubles of this world. When we meditate on God's Word and focus on His faithfulness, His peace fills our hearts.

Key Scripture:

"Set your minds on things above, not on earthly things." – Colossians 3:2

When we focus on God's perspective rather than our own limited understanding, His peace becomes more evident in our lives.

3.2. Live in the Present Moment

Many of us worry about the future or dwell on the past, but true peace is found in the present moment. Jesus taught us not to worry about tomorrow, but to trust God for today's needs.

Key Scripture:

"Therefore do not worry about tomorrow, for tomorrow will worry about itself. Each day has enough trouble of its own." – Matthew 6:34

Focusing on today and trusting God with tomorrow allows us to walk in His peace.

3.3. Practice Gratitude

Gratitude opens the door to peace. When we focus on what God has already done for us and give thanks, our hearts are filled with His peace. Gratitude shifts our focus from lack to abundance, from worry to trust.

Key Scripture:

"Give thanks in all circumstances; for this is God's will for you in Christ Jesus." – 1 Thessalonians 5:18

A heart of thanksgiving is a heart at peace.

4. The Peace of God in Difficult Circumstances

While God's peace is a gift, it doesn't mean that we won't experience trials. However, it does mean that we can experience peace in the midst of difficulty. The Apostle Paul wrote about having peace even in prison, knowing that his situation was in God's hands.

4.1. Peace in Suffering

When we experience suffering, we can still have peace because we know that God is with us and that He is using our trials to grow us. Suffering is not the absence of peace, but rather an opportunity for us to lean more deeply into God's presence.

Key Scripture:

"In all this you greatly rejoice, though now for a little while you may have had to suffer grief in all kinds of trials. These have come so that the proven genuineness of your faith—of greater worth than gold, which perishes even though refined by fire—may result in praise, glory and honor when Jesus Christ is revealed." – 1 Peter 1:6-7

4.2. Peace in the Storms of Life

Jesus showed us that peace is not dependent on external circumstances but on His presence. When the disciples were caught in a storm, Jesus calmed the waters and gave them peace, even in the midst of the chaos.

Key Scripture:

"Then he got up and rebuked the wind and the waves, and it was completely calm. The men were amazed and asked, 'What kind of man is this? Even the winds and the waves obey him!'" – Matthew 8:26-27

We can have peace even when the storms rage around us because Jesus is with us in the storm.

5. The Fruit of Walking in God's Peace

Walking in God's peace produces fruit in our lives. When we choose to trust in God and walk in His peace, we begin to reflect His character more fully.

5.1. Peace with Others

The peace we experience with God enables us to be peacemakers with others. As we walk in His peace, we become instruments of peace in a broken world.

Key Scripture:

"Blessed are the peacemakers, for they will be called children of God." – Matthew 5:9

5.2. Inner Calm in the Midst of Conflict

When we walk in God's peace, we experience inner calm even in the midst of conflict. This peace acts as a guard for our hearts, keeping us from reacting impulsively or in anger.

Key Scripture:

"Let the peace of Christ rule in your hearts, since as members of one body you were called to peace. And be thankful." – Colossians 3:15

Personal Reflection Questions

1. How do you experience the peace of God in your daily life?

2. What circumstances in your life currently challenge your peace? How can you bring those concerns to God in prayer?

3. How can you be a peacemaker in your relationships and community?

Application: Walking in God's Peace Daily

1. Take Time to Be Still

In the midst of life's busyness, set aside time to be still before God. Let His peace fill you as you quiet your mind and heart in His presence.

2. Release Worry to God

When worry arises, immediately surrender it to God in prayer. Trust Him with your concerns, and allow His peace to guard your heart.

Study Guide: "Walking in God's Peace"

Memory Verse: John 14:27

"Peace I leave with you; my peace I give you. I do not give to you as the world gives. Do not let your hearts be troubled and do not be afraid."

Daily Reading Plan:

- Day 1: John 14:27 – The promise of peace

- Day 2: Philippians 4:6-7 – Peace through prayer

- Day 3: Colossians 3:15 – Letting the peace of Christ rule in your heart

- Day 4: Isaiah 26:3 – Peace through trusting God

- Day 5: Matthew 6:25-34 – Trusting God for today

Discussion Questions:

1. What are some practical ways you can walk in God's peace every day?

2. How has the peace of God helped you in difficult times?

3. What are some specific areas where you need to trust God more fully for peace?

Conclusion: Embracing God's Peace

God's peace is a gift that we can experience daily as we trust in Him and focus on His presence. It's not based on our circumstances, but on the truth that God is in control. By walking in His peace, we reflect His character to the world around us, becoming instruments of His peace in a chaotic world.

CHAPTER 13

Living with Purpose

One of the most fulfilling aspects of the Christian journey is discovering and living out God's purpose for our lives. We were not created by accident, nor were we meant to wander aimlessly through life. God has a specific plan for each of us, one that brings Him glory and fulfills His purpose in the world. In this chapter, we will explore what it means to live with purpose, how we can discover God's purpose for our lives, and how living according to that purpose brings lasting fulfillment.

1. Understanding God's Purpose for Your Life

The first step in living with purpose is understanding that you were created with a divine purpose. God's purpose for our lives is unique to each of us, but it is always aligned with His ultimate will for the world.

Key Scripture:

"For I know the plans I have for you, declares the Lord, plans for welfare and not for evil, to give you a future and a hope."
– Jeremiah 29:11

God has plans for each of us, and those plans are good. They are filled with hope and designed to prosper us, even in difficult circumstances.

Key Scripture:

"For we are his workmanship, created in Christ Jesus for good works, which God prepared beforehand, that we should walk in them." – Ephesians 2:10

God has created us for good works—things that He has prepared for us to do before we were even born. Discovering and walking in these works is part of fulfilling His purpose for our lives.

2. Discovering Your Purpose

While God's ultimate purpose for every believer is to glorify Him, each person has unique gifts, passions, and experiences that shape how they live that purpose out. Discovering your purpose involves seeking God through prayer, studying His Word, and using your gifts to serve others.

2.1. Seek God through Prayer and Scripture

The first step in discovering God's purpose for your life is to spend time with Him in prayer and Scripture. When we seek God, He reveals more of His will to us.

Key Scripture:

"If any of you lacks wisdom, let him ask of God, who gives to all liberally and without reproach, and it will be given to him." – James 1:5

Asking God for wisdom and guidance is essential in discovering His specific plan for our lives. God delights in revealing His purpose to us when we earnestly seek Him.

2.2. Identify Your Gifts and Passions

God has given each of us unique gifts and talents that are meant to be used for His glory. These gifts are often clues to the specific purpose God has for our lives. Take time to reflect on what you are passionate about and where your natural talents lie. Often, God uses these things to guide us toward our calling.

Key Scripture:

"As each has received a gift, use it to serve one another, as good stewards of God's varied grace." – 1 Peter 4:10

2.3. Look for Opportunities to Serve

God often reveals our purpose through the opportunities He places in front of us. Serving others in practical ways—whether in the church, community, or workplace—can open the door to understanding God's calling for our lives.

Key Scripture:

"Do nothing from selfish ambition or conceit, but in humility count others more significant than yourselves." – Philippians 2:3

Service to others is a key part of fulfilling God's purpose. As we serve, God shapes our hearts and directs us toward His plan.

3. Living in Alignment with Your Purpose

Once you discover your purpose, it is important to live in alignment with it. This means making daily decisions that reflect your values, priorities, and calling. It's not enough to simply know your purpose; you must also live it out.

3.1. Surrendering to God's Will

Living with purpose begins with surrendering our plans to God. Often, God's purpose for our lives will look different from our own expectations. Surrendering to Him means trusting that His plans are better than our own.

Key Scripture:

"Trust in the Lord with all your heart, and do not lean on your own understanding. In all your ways acknowledge him, and he will make straight your paths." – Proverbs 3:5-6

Surrendering to God's will can be difficult, but it leads to a life that is aligned with His eternal purposes.

3.2. Embrace Your Unique Calling

Living with purpose requires embracing your unique calling. You were created to do specific things that no one else can do in the same way. God wants to use your individual story, gifts, and experiences to impact the world around you.

Key Scripture:

"For to each is given the manifestation of the Spirit for the common good." – 1 Corinthians 12:7

God equips each of us with unique gifts and abilities. Embrace the calling He has placed on your life, knowing that He has chosen you for a specific purpose.

3.3. Live with Intention

Living intentionally is key to living with purpose. This means making choices each day that reflect your values and your commitment to God's plan for your life. It's about being mindful of how you spend your time, resources, and energy.

Key Scripture:

"So, whether you eat or drink, or whatever you do, do all to the glory of God." – 1 Corinthians 10:31

Living with intention means making every aspect of our lives—big and small—reflective of our purpose to bring glory to God.

4. Overcoming Obstacles to Living with Purpose

Living with purpose is not always easy. There are many obstacles that can get in the way of fulfilling God's calling, such as fear, doubt, and distractions. However, with God's help, we can overcome these obstacles and continue walking in His purpose for our lives.

4.1. Overcoming Fear and Doubt

Fear and doubt can paralyze us from stepping out in faith. It's important to remember that God does not give us a spirit of fear, but a spirit of power, love, and self-control.

Key Scripture:

"For God gave us a spirit not of fear but of power and love and self-control." – 2 Timothy 1:7

When fear arises, remind yourself of God's promises and trust that He will equip you to fulfill His purpose.

4.2. Avoiding Distractions

The world is full of distractions that can lead us away from our purpose. Whether it's the busyness of life, material pursuits, or unhealthy relationships, distractions can prevent us from living intentionally.

Key Scripture:

"Let us throw off everything that hinders and the sin that so easily entangles, and let us run with perseverance the race marked out for us." – Hebrews 12:1

By focusing on what truly matters and staying committed to God's call, we can overcome distractions and live in alignment with our purpose.

5. The Rewards of Living with Purpose

When we live in alignment with God's purpose, there are many rewards. Not only do we experience fulfillment and peace, but we also bear fruit for the kingdom of God.

5.1. Fulfillment and Joy

Living with purpose brings a deep sense of fulfillment. Knowing that we are doing what God created us to do gives us peace and joy, even in the midst of challenges.

Key Scripture:

"You make known to me the path of life; in your presence there is fullness of joy; at your right hand are pleasures forevermore." – Psalm 16:11

5.2. Eternal Impact

When we live with purpose, we are impacting the kingdom of God in ways that will last for eternity. The work we do for God, no matter how small, has eternal value.

Key Scripture:

"Do not lay up for yourselves treasures on earth, where moth and rust destroy and where thieves break in and steal, but lay up for yourselves treasures in heaven." – Matthew 6:19-20

Living with purpose means investing in things that have eternal significance.

Personal Reflection Questions

1. What are the passions or talents God has given you that may be part of His purpose for your life?

2. How can you begin to live more intentionally in alignment with God's purpose for you?

3. What are some obstacles that are preventing you from living with purpose, and how can you overcome them?

Application: Living with Purpose Every Day

1. Reflect on Your Gifts and Calling

Spend time reflecting on your gifts and how they align with God's calling for your life. Ask God for clarity and direction.

2. Set Purposeful Goals

Set goals that align with your purpose. Whether it's in your family, work, or ministry, make decisions that reflect your commitment to living out God's plan.

Study Guide: "Living with Purpose"

Memory Verse: Jeremiah 29:11

"For I know the plans I have for you, declares the Lord, plans for welfare and not for evil, to give you a future and a hope."

Daily Reading Plan:

- Day 1: Jeremiah 29:11 – God's good plans for your life
- Day 2: Ephesians 2:10 – Created for good works
- Day 3: Proverbs 3:5-6 – Trusting God's plan
- Day 4: 1 Corinthians 10:31 – Doing everything for God's glory
- Day 5: Hebrews 12:1 – Running the race marked out for you

Discussion Questions:

1. What steps can you take today to begin living with purpose?

2. How does trusting God's plan for your life bring peace and fulfillment?

3. What obstacles do you need to overcome in order to fully embrace God's calling for your life?

Conclusion: Embracing Your God-Given Purpose

Living with purpose is not just about achieving goals or finding success. It's about aligning our lives with God's plan, trusting Him with our future, and using our unique gifts to serve others and glorify God. When we live out our purpose, we experience true fulfillment and impact the world for God's kingdom.

In the next chapter, we will explore the power of faith—how trusting God and believing in His promises can transform your lives and lead to victory in every area.

CHAPTER 14

The Power of Faith

Faith is the foundation of the Christian life. It's by faith that we receive salvation, live in victory, and experience the power of God in our daily lives. Faith is not just belief in something—it is trust and confidence in God's promises, His character, and His ability to work in our lives. In this chapter, we will explore the power of faith, how to strengthen it, and how it can transform our lives.

1. Understanding the Power of Faith

Faith is essential in every aspect of the Christian life. It is the key that unlocks the door to God's blessings and the means through which we overcome obstacles. True faith is not just a feeling or a wish—it is a confident trust in God's Word, even when we cannot see the outcome.

Key Scripture:

"Now faith is the substance of things hoped for, the evidence of things not seen." – Hebrews 11:1

Faith is the assurance of what we hope for, the certainty of what we cannot see. When we have faith, we trust in God's promises even before they are fully realized.

Key Scripture:

"For we walk by faith, not by sight." – 2 Corinthians 5:7

Faith is about trusting God's word, even when circumstances don't make sense or when we can't physically see the outcome.

2. The Role of Faith in Salvation

The starting point of our journey with God is salvation, and faith is the key to receiving the gift of eternal life. We are saved by grace through faith in Jesus Christ. This faith in Christ is the foundation for everything else we experience in the Christian life.

2.1. Saved by Faith

Salvation is not earned by works, but received by faith. It is through faith in Jesus Christ that we are made right with God and given the gift of eternal life.

Key Scripture:

"For by grace you have been saved through faith. And this is not your own doing; it is the gift of God, not a result of works, so that no one may boast." – Ephesians 2:8-9

Our salvation is a gift, and faith is the vehicle that allows us to receive it. By trusting in Jesus, we are brought into right relationship with God.

3. Strengthening Your Faith

Faith is not a one-time decision; it is a journey that requires growth and strengthening. The more we trust in God, the more our faith is built. Here are several ways to strengthen our faith:

3.1. Meditate on God's Word

The Word of God is the foundation of faith. The more we study and meditate on Scripture, the more we come to understand God's promises and the ways in which He has been faithful in the past.

Key Scripture:

"So faith comes from hearing, and hearing through the word of Christ." – Romans 10:17

The more we immerse ourselves in God's Word, the more our faith is strengthened.

3.2. Reflect on God's Faithfulness

One of the best ways to strengthen our faith is to reflect on God's past faithfulness. When we remember how God has come through for us in the past, it builds our confidence that He will continue to be faithful in the future.

Key Scripture:

"Remember the former things of old; for I am God, and there is no other; I am God, and there is none like me." – Isaiah 46:9

Reflecting on God's past actions helps us to trust Him for the future.

3.3. Pray for Increased Faith

Faith is something that can be increased through prayer. Jesus encourages us to ask for the faith we need, and God is faithful to supply it.

Key Scripture:

"And the apostles said to the Lord, 'Increase our faith!'" – Luke 17:5

Don't hesitate to ask God to increase your faith and help you trust Him more fully.

4. The Power of Faith to Overcome Challenges

Faith is not only essential for our salvation, but it also empowers us to face the challenges and difficulties of life. God's power works through our faith, and with faith, we can overcome obstacles, endure trials, and walk in victory.

4.1. Faith to Move Mountains

Jesus teaches that faith has the power to move mountains—to overcome the most difficult situations. Faith allows us to see beyond our current circumstances and tap into God's supernatural power.

Key Scripture:

"Truly, I say to you, if you have faith like a grain of mustard seed, you will say to this mountain, 'Move from here to there,' and it will move, and nothing will be impossible for you." – Matthew 17:20

Faith may start small, like a mustard seed, but its power is immense. Even a little faith can make a big impact when it is placed in the hands of God.

4.2. Faith to Endure Trials

Faith also gives us the strength to endure trials. When we face challenges, we can trust that God is with us, and that He will use the trial to strengthen our character and build our faith.

Key Scripture:

"We are afflicted in every way, but not crushed; perplexed, but not driven to despair; persecuted, but not forsaken; struck down, but not destroyed." – 2 Corinthians 4:8-9

Faith allows us to endure hardships with the confidence that God is at work in our lives, refining us and bringing us closer to Him.

4.3. Faith to Trust God's Timing

Faith also involves trusting in God's perfect timing. Often, we want God to act immediately, but faith teaches us to wait on Him, knowing that He is never late and that His plans are always better than ours.

Key Scripture:

"For the vision is yet for the appointed time; it hastens to the end—it will not lie. If it seems slow, wait for it; it will surely come; it will not delay." – Habakkuk 2:3

God's timing is perfect. Faith helps us to trust in His timing, even when we don't understand it.

5. The Fruits of Faith

When we live by faith, it produces fruit in our lives. Faith transforms us and leads to a fruitful life—a life that honors God and impacts the world for His kingdom.

5.1. Peace and Confidence

Faith brings peace and confidence, knowing that God is in control of our lives and that He works all things together for good. We can rest in His peace, no matter the circumstances.

Key Scripture:

"Do not be anxious about anything, but in everything by prayer and supplication with thanksgiving let your requests be made known to God. And the peace of God, which surpasses all understanding, will guard your hearts and your minds in Christ Jesus." – Philippians 4:6-7

Faith leads to peace, knowing that God is working on our behalf.

5.2. Acts of Love and Service

Faith motivates us to love others and serve them selflessly. When we have faith in God's love and provision, we are free to serve others without fear or hesitation.

Key Scripture:

"For in Christ Jesus neither circumcision nor uncircumcision counts for anything, but only faith working through love." – Galatians 5:6

Faith empowers us to love and serve others as Christ has loved us.

6. The Challenge of Living by Faith

Living by faith is not always easy. There will be times when doubts and fears creep in, and the circumstances around us may seem overwhelming. However, the Bible encourages us to stand firm in faith, knowing that God will see us through.

6.1. Faith in the Face of Doubt

Doubts are a natural part of the Christian journey, but they do not have to control us. When doubts arise, we can turn to God's Word and remind ourselves of His promises.

Key Scripture:

"But when he asked, he must believe and not doubt, because the one who doubts is like a wave of the sea, blown and tossed by the wind." – James 1:6

Faith in God's promises can overcome doubts and uncertainty.

6.2. Keep Your Eyes on Jesus

To live by faith, we must keep our eyes fixed on Jesus, the author and perfecter of our faith. He is our ultimate example of trust and obedience, and by focusing on Him, we are strengthened in our faith.

Key Scripture:

"Let us fix our eyes on Jesus, the author and perfecter of our faith, who for the joy set before him endured the cross, scorning its shame, and sat down at the right hand of the throne of God." – Hebrews 12:2

When we focus on Jesus, our faith grows stronger, and we can overcome any challenge.

Personal Reflection Questions

1. In what areas of your life do you need to strengthen your faith?

2. How has God shown His faithfulness to you in the past?

3. What challenges in your life require you to trust God more deeply?

Application: Living by Faith Every Day

1. Choose Faith Over Fear

Whenever fear or doubt arises, choose to respond with faith. Remind yourself of God's promises and trust that He is in control.

2. Step Out in Faith

Take practical steps of faith, even if it means stepping out of your comfort zone. Trust that God will guide you as you take those steps.

Study Guide: "The Power of Faith"

Memory Verse: Hebrews 11:1

"Now faith is the substance of things hoped for, the evidence of things not seen."

Daily Reading Plan:

- Day 1: Hebrews 11:1 – Understanding faith
- Day 2: Romans 10:17 – Faith comes through hearing
- Day 3: James 1:6 – Faith without doubting
- Day 4: Philippians 4:6-7 – The peace of God through faith

• Day 5: Matthew 17:20 – The power of small faith

Discussion Questions:

1. How does your faith affect the way you live your life?

2. What specific promises of God can you trust in today to strengthen your faith?

3. What steps can you take to overcome doubt and walk in greater faith?

CHAPTER 15

The Process of waiting On God

1. The Purpose of Waiting

Waiting is not wasted time. God has a purpose for every delay. Whether it's waiting for a breakthrough, healing, a relationship, a job, or an answer to prayer, God is using the waiting period to refine and strengthen us.

Key Scripture:

"But they who wait for the Lord shall renew their strength; they shall mount up with wings like eagles; they shall run and not be weary; they shall walk and not faint." – Isaiah 40:31

God promises to renew our strength as we wait on Him. Instead of becoming weary, we are strengthened spiritually when we learn to trust in His timing.

Why Does God Make Us Wait?

1. To Build Our Faith – Faith is trusting God's timing even when we don't understand it. (Hebrews 11:6)

2. To Develop Patience and Character – Waiting produces endurance and shapes our hearts. (Romans 5:3-4)

3. To Align Our Desires with His Will – Sometimes, we need to grow into what we are asking for. (Psalm 37:4)

4. To Protect Us from Rushing into the Wrong Things – God knows what's best and will not allow us to receive something before we are ready. (Proverbs 3:5-6)

2. The Challenges of Waiting

Waiting can be difficult because it challenges our trust in God. The longer the wait, the more we may feel discouraged, frustrated, or even abandoned.

2.1. The Battle Against Doubt and Fear

Doubt often creeps in when we don't see immediate results. We may wonder:

- Did God hear my prayers?

- Is He really working on my behalf?

- What if I never get what I'm waiting for?

Key Scripture:

"Wait for the Lord; be strong, and let your heart take courage; wait for the Lord!" – Psalm 27:14

God reminds us to be strong and take courage because He is always working, even when we don't see it.

2.2. Impatience and Taking Matters into Our Own Hands

Sometimes, we try to force the outcome instead of waiting for God's perfect timing. This can lead to mistakes, stress, and regret.

Example: Abraham and Sarah

God promised Abraham and Sarah a son, but when the waiting became too long, Sarah took matters into her own hands and had Abraham conceive a child with Hagar (Genesis 16). This decision led to conflict and complications that could have been avoided by waiting on God.

Key Scripture:

"Trust in the Lord with all your heart, and do not lean on your own understanding. In all your ways acknowledge him, and he will make straight your paths." – Proverbs 3:5-6

When we surrender to God's timing, we can avoid unnecessary struggles and walk in His perfect plan.

3. How to Wait on God Faithfully

Waiting is not just about sitting still—it's about actively trusting God and preparing for His answer. Here's how:

3.1. Pray and Seek God Continually

Instead of worrying, bring your concerns to God in prayer. He wants to hear from you and give you peace in the waiting process.

Key Scripture:

"Do not be anxious about anything, but in everything by prayer and supplication with thanksgiving let your requests be made known to God." – Philippians 4:6

3.2. Stay in God's Word

The Bible reminds us of God's faithfulness and strengthens our hope.

Key Scripture:

"For whatever was written in former days was written for our instruction, that through endurance and the encouragement of the Scriptures we might have hope." – Romans 15:4

3.3. Keep Serving and Growing Spiritually

Waiting doesn't mean doing nothing. Continue to serve God, grow in your faith, and prepare for what He has in store.

Example: Joseph in Egypt

Joseph waited years for God's promise to be fulfilled, but during that time, he remained faithful. Even when he was in prison, he used his gifts and served faithfully, which ultimately led to his promotion (Genesis 39-41).

4. Trusting God's Timing

God's timing is always perfect. What seems like a delay to us is actually a part of His divine plan.

4.1. God's Delays Are Not Denials

Just because something is taking longer than expected doesn't mean God has said "no." Sometimes, He is saying "not yet" because He is preparing something better.

Key Scripture:

"For the vision is yet for the appointed time; it hastens to the end—it will not lie. If it seems slow, wait for it; it will surely come; it will not delay." – Habakkuk 2:3

4.2. Rest in God's Faithfulness

Remember that God has always been faithful in the past, and He will be faithful again.

Key Scripture:

"The Lord is good to those who wait for him, to the soul who seeks him." – Lamentations 3:25

Personal Reflection Questions

1. What are you currently waiting on God for?

2. How do you usually respond when things don't happen in your timing?

3. What can you do to grow spiritually during your waiting season?

4. Have you ever taken matters into your own hands instead of waiting on God? What was the result?

Application: Making the Most of Your Waiting Season

1. Replace Worry with Worship

Instead of focusing on what you don't have yet, focus on God's faithfulness and goodness.

2. Keep a Prayer Journal

Write down your prayers and how God answers them over time. This will help you see His hand at work.

3. Find a Waiting Partner

Have someone in your life who encourages you to stay strong in faith while you wait.

Study Guide: "The Process of Waiting on God"

Memory Verse:

"Isaiah 40:31 – But they who wait for the Lord shall renew their strength; they shall mount up with wings like eagles; they shall run and not be weary; they shall walk and not faint."

Daily Reading Plan:

- Day 1: Isaiah 40:31 – Strength in waiting

- Day 2: Psalm 27:14 – Be strong and wait for the Lord

- Day 3: Proverbs 3:5-6 – Trust God's timing

- Day 4: Romans 15:4 – Find encouragement in Scripture

- Day 5: Lamentations 3:25 – The Lord is good to those who wait

Discussion Questions:

1. Why do you think God sometimes makes us wait for things?

2. What are some ways you can stay faithful while waiting?

3. How does looking at past examples of God's faithfulness help you trust His timing?

Conclusion

Waiting on God is not easy, but it is always worth it. The waiting season is not just about receiving what we're asking for—it's about becoming the person God wants us to be. If we wait with faith, patience, and trust, we will see God's promises come to pass in His perfect timing.

God is never late. Keep waiting, keep trusting, and keep growing. He's not through with you yet—it's a process!

CHAPTER 16

Overcoming Fear With Faith

Fear is one of the greatest barriers to living a life of faith. It keeps us from stepping into God's promises, fulfilling our purpose, and trusting in His plan. Fear can paralyze us, causing us to doubt God and shrink back from opportunities He has placed before us. However, the Bible repeatedly tells us, "Do not fear." In this chapter, we will explore how to overcome fear through faith, trusting God completely even in uncertain situations.

1. Understanding Fear: Where Does It Come From?

Fear entered the world through sin. In the Garden of Eden, when Adam and Eve disobeyed God, they experienced fear for the first time and hid from Him (Genesis 3:10). Ever since, fear has been one of the enemy's primary weapons to keep us from walking in God's truth.

Key Scripture:

"For God has not given us a spirit of fear, but of power and of love and of a sound mind." – 2 Timothy 1:7

Fear does not come from God—it is a tool of the enemy. God gives us power, love, and a sound mind so that we can face life with confidence.

Common Fears We Struggle With

1. Fear of the Future – Worrying about what will happen next.

2. Fear of Failure – Afraid to step out in faith because of the possibility of failing.

3. Fear of Rejection – Seeking approval from others instead of God.

4. Fear of Change – Hesitating to embrace new seasons because of uncertainty.

5. Fear of Lack – Worrying about not having enough provision or resources.

While fear is natural, it is not meant to control us. Faith is the antidote to fear.

2. How Faith Overcomes Fear

Faith is trusting in God's character, promises, and power, even when circumstances seem uncertain. The more we place our faith in God, the less power fear has over us.

2.1. Faith Reminds Us of God's Presence

Fear often comes when we feel alone or uncertain, but God is always with us.

Key Scripture:

"Fear not, for I am with you; be not dismayed, for I am your God; I will strengthen you, I will help you, I will uphold you with my righteous right hand." – Isaiah 41:10

When we remember that God is by our side, fear loses its grip.

2.2. Faith Declares God's Promises Over Fear

God's Word is filled with promises that counteract fear. When we focus on His truth instead of our worries, our faith grows stronger.

Key Scripture:

"When I am afraid, I put my trust in you. In God, whose word I praise—in God I trust and am not afraid. What can mere mortals do to me?" – Psalm 56:3-4

Speaking and believing God's promises helps us replace fear with confidence.

2.3. Faith Empowers Us to Step Forward

Fear keeps us stuck, but faith moves us forward in obedience to God.

Example: Peter Walking on Water

In Matthew 14:28-31, Peter stepped out of the boat and walked on water toward Jesus. As long as his eyes were on Jesus, he walked by faith. But when he focused on the wind and waves, he began to sink.

Lesson: Keeping our eyes on Jesus helps us overcome fear and move forward in faith.

3. Practical Steps to Overcome Fear with Faith

3.1. Pray and Give Your Fears to God

Instead of letting fear control your thoughts, bring it to God in prayer.

Key Scripture:

"Do not be anxious about anything, but in everything by prayer and supplication with thanksgiving let your requests be made known to God." – Philippians 4:6

Prayer shifts our focus from fear to faith.

3.2. Meditate on God's Word

God's Word is our greatest weapon against fear. When we fill our minds with His promises, fear loses its power.

Key Scripture:

"Your word is a lamp to my feet and a light to my path." – Psalm 119:105

3.3. Take Small Steps of Faith

Overcoming fear requires action. Start by taking small steps of obedience, even when you feel afraid.

Key Scripture:

"Be strong and courageous. Do not be afraid; do not be discouraged, for the Lord your God will be with you wherever you go." – Joshua 1:9

Faith grows when we step out in obedience.

3.4. Surround Yourself with Faith-Filled People

The people we surround ourselves with can either feed our fear or strengthen our faith. Find a community that encourages you to trust in God.

Key Scripture:

"Therefore encourage one another and build one another up, just as you are doing."

CHAPTER 17

The Power Of Surrendering To God

One of the most challenging yet rewarding aspects of the Christian journey is learning to fully surrender to God. Surrender is not a sign of weakness—it is an act of trust and obedience. When we surrender, we acknowledge that God's ways are higher than ours and that His plans are better than anything we could create on our own.

In this chapter, we will explore what it truly means to surrender, why it is necessary, and how surrendering to God brings freedom, peace, and divine direction.

1. What Does It Mean to Surrender to God?

Surrendering to God means yielding control to Him and trusting that He knows what is best for our lives. It is choosing faith over fear, obedience over personal desires, and God's will over our own plans.

Key Scripture:

"Commit your way to the Lord; trust in Him, and He will act." – Psalm 37:5

When we commit our plans, desires, and lives to God, He guides us in the right direction.

Biblical Examples of Surrender

1.Jesus in the Garden of Gethsemane

•Before going to the cross, Jesus prayed, "Father, if You are willing, take this cup from me; yet not my will, but Yours be done." – Luke 22:42

•Even in His suffering, Jesus surrendered completely to the Father's will.

2.Abraham and Isaac

•God tested Abraham's faith by asking him to sacrifice Isaac (Genesis 22). Abraham surrendered to God's command, and at the last moment, God provided a ram as a substitute.

•Lesson: Surrender leads to God's provision.

3.Mary, the Mother of Jesus

•When the angel told Mary she would give birth to Jesus, she responded, "I am the Lord's servant. May Your word to me be fulfilled." – Luke 1:38

•Lesson: Surrender requires trusting God even when we don't understand everything.

2. Why Is Surrender Necessary?

2.1. Surrender Aligns Us with God's Will

God's plans are always greater than our own. Surrendering allows His perfect will to unfold in our lives.

Key Scripture:

"For I know the plans I have for you, declares the Lord, plans for welfare and not for evil, to give you a future and a hope." – Jeremiah 29:11

2.2. Surrender Brings Freedom and Peace

Trying to control everything leads to stress and anxiety. When we surrender, we experience God's peace.

Key Scripture:

"Do not be anxious about anything, but in everything by prayer and supplication with thanksgiving let your requests be made known to God. And the peace of God, which surpasses all understanding, will guard your hearts and your minds in Christ Jesus." – Philippians 4:6-7

2.3. Surrender Strengthens Our Faith

The more we surrender, the more we learn to trust God. Faith grows when we step aside and allow God to lead.

Key Scripture:

"Trust in the Lord with all your heart, and do not lean on your own understanding. In all your ways acknowledge Him, and He will make straight your paths." – Proverbs 3:5-6

3. How to Fully Surrender to God

3.1. Let Go of Control

- Acknowledge that you don't have all the answers, but God does.

- Choose to trust Him over your own understanding.

3.2. Pray for God's Will

- Surrender begins with prayer.
- Pray daily: "Lord, not my will, but Yours be done."

3.3. Obey God's Instructions

- Surrender is not just about saying, "God, I trust You"—it's about taking action in obedience.
- Example: Peter obeyed when Jesus told him to cast his net into the water again, even after catching nothing all night (Luke 5:4-6). His obedience led to a miracle.

3.4. Release Your Worries and Desires to God

- Surrender means trusting God even when things don't go as planned.
- Replace worry with worship, knowing that God is in control.

4. The Rewards of Surrendering to God

When we surrender, we experience God's best for our lives.

4.1. Greater Clarity and Direction

- God reveals His plans when we stop resisting and start trusting.
- "The Lord will guide you always." – Isaiah 58:11

4.2. Spiritual Growth and Strength

- Surrender deepens our faith and helps us grow spiritually.

- "Remain in me, as I also remain in you. No branch can bear fruit by itself; it must remain in the vine." – John 15:4

4.3. Supernatural Peace

- No matter the situation, surrendering to God brings unshakable peace.

- "You will keep in perfect peace those whose minds are steadfast, because they trust in you." – Isaiah 26:3

Personal Reflection Questions

1. What areas of your life are hardest for you to surrender to God?

2. How has trying to control everything caused stress or worry in your life?

3. What step can you take today to practice surrendering to God's will?

4. Can you recall a time when surrendering to God led to a breakthrough?

Application: Living a Surrendered Life

1. Surrender Daily

- Each morning, pray and commit your day, plans, and worries to God.

2. Replace Worry with Worship

- When fear or doubt arise, praise God instead of stressing over the situation.

3. Take Steps of Obedience

- Don't wait until you have all the answers—act in faith and trust God's leading.

4. Surround Yourself with Faith-Filled People

- Encourage each other to trust God fully and surrender to His plans.

Study Guide: "The Power of Surrendering to God"

Memory Verse:

"Proverbs 3:5-6 – Trust in the Lord with all your heart, and do not lean on your own understanding. In all your ways acknowledge Him, and He will make straight your paths."

Daily Reading Plan:

- Day 1: Luke 22:42 – Jesus' surrender in Gethsemane
- Day 2: Jeremiah 29:11 – God's plans for our future
- Day 3: Philippians 4:6-7 – Peace through surrender
- Day 4: Proverbs 3:5-6 – Trusting God's direction
- Day 5: John 15:4 – Remaining in Christ

Discussion Questions:

1. Why is it difficult to surrender to God completely?

2.How does surrendering to God bring peace and freedom?

3.What is one thing you need to surrender to God today?

4.How does trusting in God's plan strengthen your faith?

Conclusion

Surrendering to God is not about losing—it's about gaining something greater. When we release control and trust in God's plan, we open the door to His peace, direction, and blessings.

God is not through with you yet—surrender is part of the process! Keep trusting, keep obeying, and watch how He transforms your life.

CHAPTER 18

Endurance Through Trials

Every believer will face trials, hardships, and challenges in life. The Christian walk is not free of difficulties, but God promises that He will be with us and give us the strength to endure. Endurance is a key part of spiritual growth, and through trials, God refines our faith, strengthens our character, and prepares us for greater things.

In this chapter, we will explore why God allows trials, how to endure them with faith, and the rewards of perseverance.

1. Why Does God Allow Trials?

1.1. Trials Strengthen Our Faith

Faith is like a muscle—it grows when it is tested. Without challenges, our faith remains weak.

Key Scripture:

"Consider it pure joy, my brothers and sisters, whenever you face trials of many kinds, because you know that the testing of your faith produces perseverance." – James 1:2-3

God does not allow trials to destroy us but to build us up.

1.2. Trials Help Us Rely on God

Sometimes, trials remind us that we cannot do everything on our own—we need God's strength.

Key Scripture:

"My grace is sufficient for you, for My power is made perfect in weakness." – 2 Corinthians 12:9

Instead of resisting trials, we should seek God's presence in the midst of them.

1.3. Trials Prepare Us for Greater Purpose

Joseph endured betrayal, slavery, and imprisonment before God raised him to a position of power in Egypt. His hardships prepared him to save a nation.

Key Scripture:

"You intended to harm me, but God intended it for good to accomplish what is now being done, the saving of many lives." – Genesis 50:20

The trials we go through today may be preparing us for the future.

2. How to Endure Trials with Faith

2.1. Keep Your Eyes on Jesus

When Peter walked on water, he only began to sink when he took his eyes off Jesus and focused on the storm.

Key Scripture:

"Fixing our eyes on Jesus, the pioneer and perfecter of faith. For the joy set before Him, He endured the cross." – Hebrews 12:2

No matter what we face, we must keep our focus on Christ.

2.2. Stand Firm in God's Word

God's Word is our foundation during hard times.

Key Scripture:

"Heaven and earth will pass away, but My words will never pass away." – Matthew 24:35

2.3. Pray Without Ceasing

Prayer connects us to God's strength and wisdom.

Key Scripture:

"Do not be anxious about anything, but in every situation, by prayer and petition, with thanksgiving, present your requests to God." – Philippians 4:6

2.4. Trust God's Timing

Trials are temporary, but God's promises are eternal.

Key Scripture:

"And we know that in all things God works for the good of those who love Him, who have been called according to His purpose." – Romans 8:28

3. The Rewards of Endurance

3.1. Spiritual Maturity

Endurance brings wisdom, patience, and deeper faith.

Key Scripture:

"Let perseverance finish its work so that you may be mature and complete, not lacking anything." – James 1:4

3.2. Victory Over the Enemy

The devil wants to use trials to discourage us, but when we stand firm, we overcome his attacks.

Key Scripture:

"Submit yourselves, then, to God. Resist the devil, and he will flee from you."

CHAPTER 19

Walking In The Power Of The Holy Spirit

The Christian life is not meant to be lived in our own strength. God has given us the Holy Spirit to empower, guide, and transform us. The Holy Spirit is not just a force or a feeling—He is God's presence within us, equipping us for every good work.

In this chapter, we will explore who the Holy Spirit is, how He empowers us, and how we can walk daily in His power.

1. Who Is the Holy Spirit?

The Holy Spirit is the third person of the Trinity—co-equal with God the Father and God the Son. He is not an impersonal force but a divine Helper sent to dwell in believers.

1.1. The Holy Spirit Is Our Helper

Jesus promised that the Holy Spirit would come after He ascended to heaven.

Key Scripture:

"And I will ask the Father, and He will give you another Helper, to be with you forever— the Spirit of truth." – John 14:16-17

The Holy Spirit teaches, comforts, convicts, and empowers us to live for God.

1.2. The Holy Spirit Lives in Us

When we accept Christ, the Holy Spirit comes to dwell within us.

Key Scripture:

"Do you not know that your bodies are temples of the Holy Spirit, who is in you, whom you have received from God?" – 1 Corinthians 6:19

This means we have access to God's wisdom, strength, and guidance at all times.

2. The Power of the Holy Spirit

2.1. The Holy Spirit Gives Us Power

The early disciples were afraid and uncertain until they received the Holy Spirit. Then, they became bold witnesses for Christ.

Key Scripture:

"But you will receive power when the Holy Spirit comes on you; and you will be My witnesses." – Acts 1:8

The Holy Spirit gives us the boldness to share the Gospel, strength to endure trials, and power to overcome sin.

2.2. The Holy Spirit Transforms Our Character

The Holy Spirit doesn't just give us power—He changes who we are from the inside out.

Key Scripture:

"But the fruit of the Spirit is love, joy, peace, forbearance, kindness, goodness, faithfulness, gentleness, and self-control." – Galatians 5:22-23

When we allow the Holy Spirit to lead us, our thoughts, attitudes, and behaviors reflect Christ.

2.3. The Holy Spirit Gives Us Spiritual Gifts

Every believer is given spiritual gifts to serve God and others.

Key Scripture:

"Now to each one the manifestation of the Spirit is given for the common good." – 1 Corinthians 12:7

Some of these gifts include wisdom, healing, prophecy, discernment, and speaking in tongues.

3. How to Walk in the Power of the Holy Spirit

3.1. Surrender Daily to the Holy Spirit

Instead of relying on our own strength, we must let the Holy Spirit guide our lives.

Key Scripture:

"Since we live by the Spirit, let us keep in step with the Spirit." – Galatians 5:25

3.2. Spend Time in Prayer

The more we pray, the more we are filled with the Holy Spirit's power.

Key Scripture:

"Pray in the Spirit on all occasions with all kinds of prayers and requests." – Ephesians 6:18

3.3. Obey the Holy Spirit's Leading

When the Holy Spirit prompts us, we must listen and obey.

Example: In Acts 8:29, Philip obeyed the Spirit's prompting to speak to the Ethiopian eunuch, leading to his salvation.

3.4. Walk by Faith, Not by Feelings

Even when we don't feel strong, we trust the Holy Spirit is with us.

Key Scripture:

"For we walk by faith, not by sight." – 2 Corinthians 5:7

4. The Rewards of Walking in the Spirit

When we live in the power of the Holy Spirit, we experience:

- Greater spiritual authority
- Deeper intimacy with God
- Boldness in our faith
- Victory over sin
- Direction and wisdom for life's decisions

Key Scripture:

"Now the Lord is the Spirit, and where the Spirit of the Lord is, there is freedom." – 2 Corinthians 3:17

Personal Reflection Questions

1. Have you fully surrendered to the Holy Spirit's guidance in your life?

2. In what areas do you need the Holy Spirit's power today?

3. What spiritual gifts has God given you to serve others?

4. How can you grow in your relationship with the Holy Spirit?

Application: Living a Spirit-Filled Life

1. Invite the Holy Spirit Daily

Pray each day: "Holy Spirit, fill me and guide me today."

2. Study the Word

The Holy Spirit speaks through the Bible—make time for God's Word daily.

3. Be Bold in Your Faith

Step out in faith and let the Spirit use you to impact others.

4. Stay Sensitive to the Spirit

Listen for the Holy Spirit's guidance and obey His leading.

Study Guide: "Walking in the Power of the Holy Spirit"

Memory Verse:

"Acts 1:8 – But you will receive power when the Holy Spirit comes on you; and you will be My witnesses."

Daily Reading Plan:

- Day 1: John 14:16-17 – The Holy Spirit as our Helper
- Day 2: Acts 1:8 – Receiving the Spirit's power
- Day 3: Galatians 5:22-23 – The Fruit of the Spirit
- Day 4: 1 Corinthians 12:7-11 – Spiritual gifts
- Day 5: Romans 8:14 – Being led by the Spirit

Discussion Questions:

1. How has the Holy Spirit worked in your life?

2. Why do we need the Holy Spirit's power to live as Christians?

3. What is one step you can take to walk more closely with the Holy Spirit?

4. How can you use your spiritual gifts to serve others?

Conclusion

The Holy Spirit is not just for a select few—He is available to every believer. When we surrender to Him, He empowers us to live victoriously, fulfill our purpose, and experience God's supernatural power in our daily lives.

God is not through with you yet—walking in the Spirit is part of the process! Stay filled, stay faithful, and watch what God does through you.

CHAPTER 20

He's Not Through With You Yet - Embracing the Lifelong Journey with God

As we reach the final chapter of this journey, it is time to embrace a profound truth: God's work in your life is ongoing. Every challenge, every trial, every moment of waiting and every act of faith is part of a process that transforms you into the person God intends you to be. You are not finished—He's not through with you yet! This chapter will help you celebrate the lifelong journey of faith, encourage you to continue trusting in God's process, and remind you that every step you take is part of His grand design.

1. Embracing the Journey

1.1. God's Work Is Never Complete

The Bible reminds us that God is continually working in our lives. Even when we feel worn out or uncertain, His transforming power is at work.

Key Scripture:

"Being confident of this, that He who began a good work in you will carry it on to completion until the day of Christ Jesus." – Philippians 1:6

Every season—whether of joy or pain—is a stepping stone towards spiritual maturity. Rather than seeing trials as failures or delays, we can view them as essential parts of God's refining process.

1.2. The Journey of Faith Is Lifelong

Faith is not a destination but a continuous walk with God. Our lives are filled with moments of growth, learning, and transformation.

Key Scripture:

"For we walk by faith, not by sight." – 2 Corinthians 5:7

Even when the path is unclear or the way seems long, trust that God is always at work. The journey itself shapes our character and prepares us for what lies ahead.

2. Recognizing the Signs of God's Continued Work

2.1. Transformation Through Trials

Reflect on how past challenges have shaped you. Often, what we consider setbacks are actually setups for greater breakthroughs.

Example:

Joseph's story reminds us that years of hardship and waiting led to his rise as a leader in Egypt (Genesis 37–41). His life was a testament to God's purpose unfolding over time.

2.2. Evidences of Spiritual Growth

Spiritual maturity is evident in increased patience, deeper prayer life, and a growing love for others.

Key Scripture:

"But the fruit of the Spirit is love, joy, peace, patience, kindness, goodness, faithfulness, gentleness, self-control." – Galatians 5:22-23

These fruits are not produced overnight; they are the result of God's ongoing work in our hearts.

2.3. Continuous Guidance and Provision

God's provision and guidance never cease. Even in moments of uncertainty, He equips us with the strength and wisdom needed for the next step.

Key Scripture:

"And we know that in all things God works for the good of those who love Him, who have been called according to His purpose." – Romans 8:28

3. Living with Hope and Expectation

3.1. Trusting in God's Promises

Every promise in God's Word reinforces that our story is not over. God's promises are eternal, and He is faithful to bring them to fruition in our lives.

Key Scripture:

"For I know the plans I have for you, declares the Lord, plans for welfare and not for evil, to give you a future and a hope." – Jeremiah 29:11

3.2. Keeping an Eternal Perspective

When we fix our eyes on the eternal, our present struggles take on a new meaning. We begin to understand that every experience has a purpose in God's larger plan for eternity.

Key Scripture:

"So we fix our eyes not on what is seen, but on what is unseen, since what is seen is temporary, but what is unseen is eternal." – 2 Corinthians 4:18

3.3. Encouraging Others on Their Journey

Your journey is not meant to be walked alone. Sharing your experiences of God's faithfulness can encourage others to remain steadfast in their own walk of faith.

4. Practical Steps to Embrace the Lifelong Process

4.1. Cultivate a Daily Relationship with God

Make daily time for prayer, worship, and meditation on Scripture. This daily connection is vital for continual growth.

Application Tip: Start or end each day by journaling your thoughts and the ways God has worked in your life, no matter how small they may seem.

4.2. Celebrate Small Victories

Recognize and celebrate every instance of God's faithfulness—even the little ones. Each small victory is part of the larger transformation.

Application Tip: Create a "gratitude list" where you record answered prayers and moments of joy throughout your week.

4.3. Stay Connected with a Community

Surround yourself with believers who encourage and uplift you. Their testimonies can reinforce your own hope and remind you that God is still at work in your life.

Application Tip: Join a small group or Bible study where you can share and learn from one another.

4.4. Keep Learning and Growing

Invest in spiritual growth through reading, seminars, or mentorship. The more you learn, the more you understand that the journey of faith is dynamic and ongoing.

Personal Reflection Questions

1. Reflect on a time when a trial or period of waiting ultimately led to spiritual growth. How did that experience shape you?

2. What are some signs in your life that indicate God is still actively working in you?

3. How can you encourage someone who feels stuck or discouraged in their faith journey?

4. In what ways can you intentionally nurture your relationship with God on a daily basis?

Study Guide: "He's Not Through With You Yet – Embracing the Lifelong Journey"

Memory Verse:

"Being confident of this, that He who began a good work in you will carry it on to completion until the day of Christ Jesus." – Philippians 1:6

Daily Reading Plan:

- Day 1: Philippians 1:6 – Reflect on God's promise to complete His work in you.
- Day 2: Jeremiah 29:11 – Meditate on God's plans for your future.
- Day 3: 2 Corinthians 4:18 – Focus on the eternal perspective.
- Day 4: Romans 8:28 – Understand how God works all things for your good.
- Day 5: Galatians 5:22-23 – Identify the fruits of the Spirit growing in your life.

Discussion Questions:

1. How does knowing that God's work in you is ongoing change your perspective on current challenges?

2.What practices can help you remain hopeful and expectant for what God has planned for your future?

3. In what ways can you share your journey with others to inspire and encourage them?

Conclusion: Your Journey Is Far from Over

Every chapter of your life is part of a grand narrative authored by God. Though you may face trials, doubts, and moments of uncertainty, remember that He is continually at work, refining you, strengthening your faith, and preparing you for future blessings. Embrace the journey with hope, knowing that God's promises are sure, His timing is perfect, and His work in you is far from finished.

Keep walking in faith, keep trusting in His process, and always remember—He's not through with you yet!

This final chapter is not an ending, but an invitation to continue the lifelong journey of faith. As you move forward, let the truth of God's unwavering love and purpose carry you through every season of your life. And always Remember life is a process.God Remnant Mcbean♥.

He's Not Through with You Yet – It's a Process

www.ingramcontent.com/pod-product-compliance
Lightning Source LLC
Chambersburg PA
CBHW070541170426
43200CB00011B/2507